SIGNAL 55

Volume II: Fire Trucks Fire Stations and More

Chief Jim Dorman, Retired

The Front Cover features a photo of a helmet that was previously owned by Jack deSaulles, a Boardman volunteer firefighter. Jack served from 1938 to 1955. He passed his helmet on to his son J.B. deSaulles who joined Boardman Fire Department in 1955. J.B. deSaulles rose to the rank of Assistant Chief then passed the helmet on to his stepdaughter Kathy May when she became the first female volunteer firefighter in Boardman.

The Back Cover includes a photograph taken by my children shortly before I retired. They took pictures for a photo album they created for me in celebration of my retirement. The photo was taken by placing the grandkids on the ledge used while loading hose on the ladder truck. My family is the family of a firefighter. Some endured anxiety when I was away on a serious fire. Others endured my stories of the things I had done while in the fire service.

ISBN 979-8-218-27728-4

Signal 55 is my first and probably only attempt to write a book. Here is how it began. Our historical documents had been stored over the office of the Boardman Township mechanic's building. The documents were in cardboard boxes and subject to the summer heat and the winter cold. But worst of all, the roof began to leak. These boxes were rescued and brought into the safety of the main fire station where they were kept in an open storage area. Many years ago, while I was still on the job, I looked briefly through the boxes and found a lot of journals, documents, old pictures, and scrapbooks donated by retired firefighters but nothing was organized. At the time, I had no interest in this mish mash of journals, pictures, and documents. It wasn't until later that I found there were treasures in those boxes. Information about our history that no one ever knew about.

In retirement, I realized that I enjoyed writing after creating a "Grandparent's Journal" for our kids and grandkids. Once done with that project, I suddenly knew that I needed to take this newly found pastime and apply it to the boxes of disorganized history of our department. So, I organized the boxes, found scrap books from other firefighters, and interviewed firefighters and family members. Suddenly, there was much more information about our department than was included in those boxes. I wrote for six years.

With so much material available about the history of Boardman Fire Department, it became apparent that one book would be too big. My concept of the project was to take all of the boxes of archived materials and present **all of our complete history** in one place. Based on how I conceived my mission, trimming pieces of our history from the book to make it a more acceptable size was never going to happen. The solution was that there needed to be two volumes to tell all of the stories of our history.

Volume I presents the year-by-year history of our department. Signal 55 Volume II presents all of the lists of important data and facts such as all fire trucks, the evolution of the fire stations, and many more interesting items. The two books together will provide the reader with everything that is known about the 100 year history of Boardman Fire Department.

ACKNOWLEDGEMENTS

Thanks to John Darnell for his assistance and his father Jack for all the historical pictures he took and preserved. The Mahoning Dispatch from Canfield provided data from 1917 to 1937. Thank you to Tim Seman from the Youngstown Library for his time spent researching articles and information for me. Thanks to all the people who made photos, scrapbooks, memorabilia, and anecdotes available for inclusion in the books. I would like to thank Mark Brown who approved licensing of the hundreds of photos and articles that appeared in the two books. Great volumes of Boardman Fire Department history were recorded in the Vindicator. Mark Brown was the former General Manager of the Youngstown Vindicator. His family owned and published the paper for decades.

Thank you to Jim McCreary who poured over the department's historical data before I started writing. He scanned, copied, and cataloged so many of the photos, articles, and documents. He gave me his work which saved me countless hours of research. He provided the foundation that made it easy for me to start this book!

A special thank you to Barney Davison who was 87, Bill Bush who was 86, Bob Davis who was 78, and Bill Evans who was 90 the first time I contacted them for information about the old days and the startup of our department. Thanks to Bob Wright for editing and guidance. Thank you to Penny Badolato for her artistic rendering of the first fire station.

Lastly, my wife Sandy deserves so much credit, and thanks. Without complaint, she edited and proofread time after time and found my grammar and spelling mistakes. She guided me in the presentation and helped keep the book on the path. Her assistance was a major contribution to the success of the book. Thank you so very much!

Contents

Blank Page

Boardman Junior Fire Department

On March 8, 1949, two senior firemen, T. J. Smith, and Sid Nordquist approached Chief Gifford with an idea. Let's train young men and boys in the skills of firefighting. We can gain their assistance in emergencies and help keep the teenagers out of trouble. The Chief approved and immediately eight boys, between the ages of 16 and 21, took advantage of the offer and organized the club. The Junior Firefighters organization began.

This article appearing in the Youngstown Vindicator in 1951 two years after the club's formation, provides us with the history of the Boardman Junior Fire Department.

The headline in the Youngstown Vindicator: **"Fireboys" Are Real Asset to Boardman Fire Department.**

Some of the 20 youths who are providing community service as members of the Boardman Junior Fire Department line up with fire department officers. Bob Ewing, a part-time fireman, is in the truck. Fire Chief M. W. Gifford (in white coat) and Assistant Albert Zima are at far right in the front row. BJFD members (left to right, front row) are John Craig, Dale Bradshaw, Fred Ginder, Phil Blake, Ed Bush, Dave Dyer, Myron Davis; (back row) Bob Williams, Vernon Mesmer, Claude Smoyer, Bob Ivan, Eugene MacDougall.

Twenty Boardman boys having the times of their lives doing good community service without fanfare, fuss, or favor. The 20 are members of the Boardman Junior Fire Department. They help the Boardman Fire Department on calls and can be recognized by their flaming red fire coats. Two years ago, Boardman firemen organized the Junior group and taught them something about firefighting. Today Fire Chief Merle W. Gifford says, "They are a big help to us and they would be a big help to any community." The "Junior fire-eaters" answer all calls along with the department. Of course, these boys, aged 16 to 21, are not permitted to go inside burning buildings. They direct traffic at fires, run errands, help firemen play strong pressure hoses on burning buildings, perform other chores of a fireman, and are permitted to drive the fire trucks back to the station. A blanket insurance policy covers the youths in case of injury.

The first roll call of the Boardman Junior Fire Department found John N. Craig, Robert Conklin, Thomas Evans, Douglas Newmann, Robert Mullen, Dom Sawyer, Carroll Smith, and Dean Spathold answering up. Evans was elected president. The only requirement was that the boys had to be over the age of 16 and under 21. Under training by their advisors, Albert Zima, Howard Jessop, and Gene

Mayberry, the boys learned the operations of a fire department. They began to handle all firefighting equipment and learned to operate the trucks. Their activities drew the interest of other youths and the club began to grow. All received the regular training of a fireman and the biggest moment in their lives came when they answered their first alarm. The work of the Juniors at fires surprised the seniors. Chief Gifford noted that the boys are well disciplined. "The boys have a marvelous organization and more communities should have such an organization," he declared.

Robert Ewing, left, and John N. Craig, right, members of the Boardman Junior Fire Department, couple a fire hose to the fire engine as Assistant Fire Chief Albert Zima, center, tells them how.

The seniors gave the club $25 and the boys swelled this fund to $313 by selling scrap and newspapers. Last week they bought 20 red coats for $224 and now they are as fully equipped as a regular fireman. Their helmets are made from G. I. helmet liners. They have badges inscribed "Boardman Junior Fire Department." They wear regular firemen's dress hats in parades.

When the fire alarm rings in the Boardman neighborhood, the Juniors rush to one of the two fire stations on foot or motor scooters, motorbikes, and bicycles. Parents have given approval to their sons being Junior firemen and the organization has the tacit approval of the schools. Many a Junior "fire-eater" has displayed his impatience in classrooms during a fire alarm but none has attempted to cut classes to fight a fire. One of their advisors, Zima, said "in case of a very serious fire in Boardman, I am sure the school authorities would permit the Junior firemen to leave classes. But we don't want to call them during school hours unless there is a great emergency."

Last March, the boys had a banquet to celebrate their anniversary (first year). Just as Juniors and seniors finished eating the fire alarm rang and everybody rushed to respond. Here was their big chance, but unfortunately, it was a false alarm. During the "Big Snow' last November, the Juniors rushed Mrs. Floor of 43 Erskine Avenue to the hospital and later presented her baby son with a Junior Fire Department badge and an honorary membership in their organization.

The youths have taken trips to Columbus and toured the city's fire station; they have marched in parades in Boardman, Wellsville, Petersburg, and Columbus. They have club rooms above the Number 1 fire station on Canfield Poland Road near Southern Boulevard and hold training drills every Thursday evening. Now they are studying first aid so they can assume roles in civilian defense. "It's the best thing a fellow can get into," one of the members said, "You can get into this organization to have fun and at the same time do service for the community."

"The Junior firemen have two captains who are rotated every six months. Right now, Daniel Feicht and Edwin F. Beede are captains until July 1 when 2 new captains will be appointed. The president of the club is Edwin C. Bush. Other officers are Ed Feicht, vice president; Robert Conklin, secretary; and John N. Craig, treasurer. One of the former members, Robert Ewing, is now a part-time member of the senior fire department and acts as a senior club advisor."

Bill Bush said that the Juniors never drilled with the senior firefighters. When asked how they melded together from two separate groups Bill replied, "In part from picnics and banquets they were invited to but primarily they learned to work together when they showed up at the actual fire scenes to help out."

This picture was taken in 1949. Only four of the Juniors can be identified. Standing from left to right are Buster Davis, Ed Beede, and Bob Bayne. Kneeling second from the right is J.B. deSaulles.

The Juniors in the basement of 136 Boardman Poland Road preparing for dinner and the cleanup afterward.

This picture was taken in 1951.

(L-R) Back Row: Bob Bayne, John Bradshaw, Ed Bush, Doug Newman, Dale Bradshaw
Center Row: Donald Feicht, John B deSaulles, Gene MacDougall, Bob Ewing
Front Row: Gene Mayberry, Al Zima, Ed Beede, Buster Davis, Vern Mesmer, Howard Jessop, Chief Merle Gifford

Initially, there were 8 members between the ages of 16 and 21. It was likely that a force of junior firefighters would augment the depleted membership of the senior firefighters as numerous men went off to support the war effort.

The first members of the Junior Firefighters were:

- John Craig
- Robert Conklin
- Thomas Evans, the first President
- Douglas Newman
- Dom Sawyer
- Caroll Smith
- Dean Spathold

BOARDMAN JUNIOR FIRE DEPARTMENT
CONSTITUTION

FRED HOOVER

Preamble — I as a member of the Boardman Junior Fire Department do solemnly swear to obey all the rules and regulations of the Boardman Fire Department. I will assist my Senior Firemen at all times to the best of my ability.

Article 1 — The purpose of this club is to train its members in the field of Fire Service. The secondary purpose shall be social.

Article 2 — Qualifications of the applicant.

A. Applicant must be between the ages of 16 and 21 to join the club. There is no age maximum for remaining in the club.
B. Applicant shall state any physical disabilities he may have.

Article 3 — Application and probation.

A. Application must be filed before acceptance into the club, and furthermore no probationist may attend any fire, drill or any other activities except meetings until the form for relieving the Township Trustees, and The Fire Department of any obligations is signed by the applicants parents.
B. All aplicants will be required to attend four (4) meetings. These meetings will be required in succession on part of the applicant.
C. Immediately after acceptance into the club a helmet shall be issued. After eight (8) weeks a member is entitled to full equipement.
   1. Full equipment shall consist of Raincoat, Helmet, Boots, Dress Hat, Hat badge, Shirt badge, and Tie.
D. All probationist are voted on by secret ballot. Majority of those present is required. Totals of of these ballots shall be shown to those who voted.
E. All probationists shall be required to pay a $1.25 membership fee upon acceptance into the club.

Article 4 — Duties of members.

A. Members shall attend all meetings unless excused by the advisor having that meeting.
B. Any member missing three (3) meetings in succession without reasonable excuse which shall be determined by an advisor may be boted out. However a warning of one week prior to the vote is customary.
C. Any member missing one meeting without reasonable excuse which will be determined by the club will be assesed a fine of $.75 and suspended by the club until fine is paid.
D All members must be present at any important meeting that is announced beforehand.
E. Members _must_ be present and wear _clean_ clothes to all social meetings.
F. Members _must_ support _all_ outside activities.
G. Full dress uniform shall be worn to all outside activities unless otherwise designated.
   1. Outside activities shall consist of parades, parking cars, etc.
H. Full dress uniform shall include: Uniform jacket,

White shirt, Black Tie, White socks, Dark (blue or black) unpegged pants, Dress hat, Hat badge, Shirt badge, and unpointed Black Shoes.

I. All members will not do anything outside of meetings that would reflect on the Senior or Junior Departments. Anyone doing so may be expelled or suspended upon an advisor's advice.

J. All equipment must be returned to the club when a member leaves.

K. Any member talking out of turn or acting disorderly at a meeting shall be fined by the Seargent-of-Arms. If fined a third time during the same meeting he shall be excused from that meeting, and any following activities until the fine is paid.

L. Members shall pay dues of $.75 a month. Any member being delinquent three (3) months dues may be suspended by a vote of the club.

Article 5 Officers and their duties.

A. Chief: shall be in charge of the Juniors at fires, drills, and all outside activities.

B. Assistant Chief: shall keep a record of distributing, collecting, and the storing of all the Junior Fire Dept. equipment. He shall also be in charge of the point system, and take the duties of the chief when the chief is not present.

C. President: shall conduct meetings, and appoint all committees, he shall appoint the Sergent-at-Arms. He shall have the power to vote only in case of a tie.

D. Vice-President: shall conduct one meeting each month.

E. Treasurer: shall make all finiancial transactions and keep an up to date record.

F. Secretary: shall keep attendance, minutes, and a roster of all active and honary members.

G. Corresponding Secretary: shall make all correspondence for the club. Correspondence shall consist of all letters and phone calls to all its members concerning activities of the club.

H. Elections are to be held every six months (6), Preferably the first week in January and July, however an election may be called anytime that it is needed.

Article 6 Point System:

A. The point system is a system whereby this club functions. From this system members are qualified to hold office and to retain membership.

B. Points shall be distributed for the following activities:

1. Fires- 5 points for the first hour. For each additional hour five (5) points will also be given.
2. Drills- 5 points for each drill no hourly measurement.
3. Parking cars- 5 points for each time.
4. Parades- 2 points.
5. Mahoning Valley meetings 3 points.
6. Juniors meetings- 3 points.
7. Tests

95-100 = 5 points	60-70 = -1 point
90-95 = 4 points	50-60 = -2 points
85-90 = 3 points	45-50 = -3 points
80-85 = 2 points	40-45 = -4 points
70-80 = 1 point	0-40 = -5 points

C. Members must have half year totals of 100 points to remain in the club.
D. Members must have half year totals of 150 points to eligible for office.
E. The chief, Asst. Chief, and an advisor shall determine extra points to be given.

Article 7 Suspension or Expulsion.

A. The Chief may give one week suspension with an advisors permission. After this week is up the club may vote an additional suspension.
B. Suspension may be given for the following:
   1. Disobeying an order at a fire or drill.
   2. Misconduct at the fire station or anywhere that it would reflect on the Juniors or the Fire Dept.
   3. Not showing up for a special activity, when your appearance has been promised.

Article 8 Fire Reports:

A. Fire reports MUST be filled out the same day as the fire.
B. All reports are to be filled out in ink.
C. A fireman on duty at the time of the fire or drill must sign the report or it is not valid and will be destroyed.

The advisors were: Gene Mayberry, Albert Zima, and Howard Jessop.

A January 1953 Vindicator article mentions the following members: John Bradshaw President, Vern Mesmer Vice President, John (J.B.) deSaulles Secretary and Chief of the Juniors, Don Mauch Treasurer, Myron Davis Assistant Chief, Don Feight, and Ed Beede.

In 1954, the following people were listed as Honorary Members of the Juniors: Bob Bayne, Bill Bush, and John Craig. These three young men likely joined the Armed Forces.

March 1955 was the 6th anniversary of the Junior's organization. J.B. deSaulles was the Chief. It was reported that Chuck Vimerstedt of the Greater Youngstown Safety Council went to a Scouting round table on the organization and operation of a Junior Fire Department as a supplement to Scouting. He was accompanied by J. B. deSaulles.

In March of 1956, at a banquet to celebrate the 7th year of a Junior Fire Department, J.B. deSaulles was presented with an Ex-Chief's gold badge honoring his five terms as Chief which ended when he was appointed to the full-paid department in July of 1955. deSaulles was appointed at the age of 18. At the same time, Alfred (Barney) Davison was appointed on a full-time basis. The two men replaced Don Neapolitan and Fred Huston who resigned.

In March of 1958, it was the Junior's 9th year. Don Mauch was the club President of the Juniors. Bob Wright joined the Juniors in 1962 at the age of 16. Wright joined at the same time as Dave Carlson and Phil Ensley. These three boys were the last young men to join the Junior organization. Wright also remembers Lynn White and John Marsh along with Rocky Shaw and Gary Wunderlin. These were the only Juniors remaining. The firefighters from the Boardman Volunteer Fire Company could no longer recruit members to join the Junior Firefighters. The membership numbers began to fade as Juniors were placed on the volunteer organization. Wright joined the volunteers in 1964 at the age of 18. When it came to fire gear, the volunteers were told to go through the pile of used protective clothing that had been discarded by the paid men as their clothing had been updated. Wright was dissatisfied with the quality of fire gear in the leftover pile so he chose to buy his own. His bunker coat was priced at $32.80 in 1965. Today, a fire coat can cost $1,800 or more.

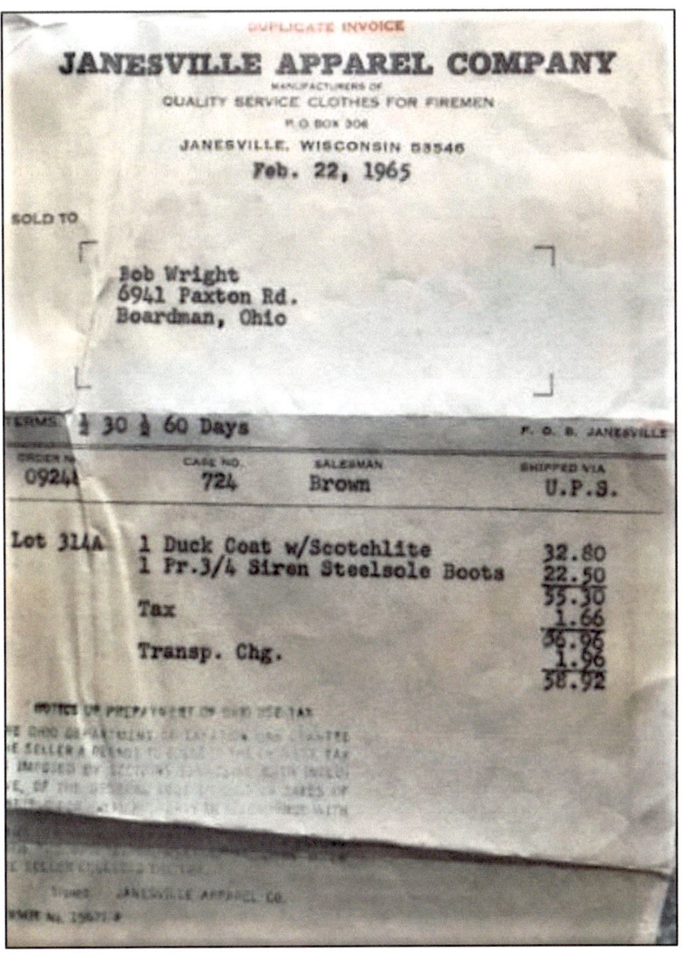

DUPLICATE INVOICE

JANESVILLE APPAREL COMPANY

MANUFACTURERS OF
QUALITY SERVICE CLOTHES FOR FIREMEN
P.O. BOX 306
JANESVILLE, WISCONSIN 53546

Feb. 22, 1965

SOLD TO

Bob Wright
6941 Paxton Rd.
Boardman, Ohio

TERMS ½ 30 ½ 60 Days F. O. B. JANESVILLE

ORDER No.	CASE NO.	SALESMAN	SHIPPED VIA
0924	724	Brown	U.P.S.

Lot 314A	1 Duck Coat w/Scotchlite	32.80
	1 Pr.3/4 Siren Steelsole Boots	22.50
		55.30
	Tax	1.66
		56.96
	Transp. Chg.	1.96
		58.92

JANESVILLE APPAREL CO.

The Bangor Ladders. The Juniors were trained in the proper and safe way to raise and lower the bangor ladder. A four-man group used very precise orders to make the operation run smoothly. One firefighter took command and gave orders such as, "Prepare to Raise, Raise, Prepare to Set, Set, Prepare to Take Down, Take Down, Take Down, Prepare to Lower and Lower." This ensured an efficient and safe use of the ladder. The house seen in these pictures was located on Market Street at Gertrude Avenue.

In an interview, John Craig told, "On March 8, 1949, I joined the Junior firefighters and became one of the founding members." He said in the beginning, "There was a group of teenage boys who hung around Perry's Gas Station and the fire station across the street. Steve Perry didn't want them around since they were "raisin hell and pitching pennies against the wall." The boys had shown some interest in what the firemen did so members of the fire department devised a way to keep the boys out of trouble and do something useful. They decided to form a group and teach the boys firefighting. Originally, the youth organization was supposed to be a Boy Scout Explorers group but that didn't work out so the firemen formed the Boardman Junior Firefighters Club. Howard Jessop and Al Zima were the first advisors for the club.

Their first uniforms were the soft dress hat with a Junior firefighter emblem for the hat and a Junior firefighter badge. Fire gear included a rubber coat, pull-up boots, and a plastic helmet with a shield on the front." Craig said, "One of the Neapolitan brothers made a plaque for the wall that had crossed axes and nozzles at the top and listed the names of the first members." The boys formalized matters by electing a President, held regular meetings, and participated in weekly training events. The first fundraising effort by the boys was collecting scrap metal. Smith Dairy loaned the boys one of the spare trucks to help them collect the scrap. They also parked cars at football and basketball games.

Craig said, "The boys were the first to take the State-certified 36 hour firefighter course. We trained by ourselves without the senior firemen. We were better than them old guys." But despite their confidence, Juniors were not allowed to fight fires inside the buildings. They had to remain outside. Bill Bush lived down the street from him and when a fire call came in, Bush would pick Craig up on his Cushman and the two of them would race to the fire on the scooter. If he couldn't catch a ride with someone, he rode his bike to fire calls. He remembers fighting fires from outside of the building and pumping cellars in the 1950 flood for 39 hours.

Craig left the Juniors and joined the military service in 1952. After his tour of duty was up, he put in a letter of application for the Boardman volunteers but according to him, "didn't make the vote." So, he moved to Canfield and joined their fire department. John Craig was with the safety department at Ohio Edison. He gave many electrical safety classes to Boardman firefighters throughout the eighties and nineties.

Junior Firefighter Roster

I have examined all articles and personal stories about the Juniors in search of the names of members. Listed are all that I have been able to locate. Bob Bayne, Edwin Beede, Howard Bieber, Phil Blake, Dale Bradshaw, John Bradshaw, Bill Bush, Ed Bush, Jim Carlo, Dave Carlson, Robert Conklin, John Craig, Myron Davis, Buster Davis, Robert Davis, John deSaulles, Jack DeVine, Dave Dyer, Phil Ensley, Thomas Evans, Bob Ewing, Daniel Feicht, Donald Feicht, Don Fisher, Fred Ginder, Fred Hoover, Bob Ivan, Eugene MacDougal, John Marsh, Don Mauch, LeRoy Mayberry, Larry Mayberry, Jim McCarty, Vern Mesmer, Tony Minicuicci, Robert Mullen, Don Neapolitan, Jack Neapolitan, Douglas Newman, Doug Nybell, Bill Parker, Bob Rauchenback, Dom Sawyer, Harold (Rocky) Shaw, Caroll Smith, Claude Smoyer, Dean Spathold, Lynn White, Bob Williams, Wayne Williams, Bob Wright, Gary Winderlin.

✠ *The Variety Shows* ✠

Boardman Fire Department used variety shows for several decades to raise funds for the department. The following pictures are from one of the Boardman Volunteer Firefighter's shows held in the late 1940s. The firefighters put on a show annually starting from the department's earliest days.

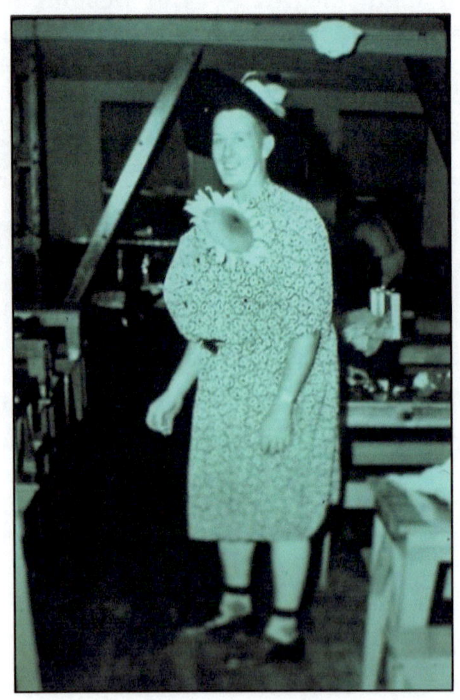

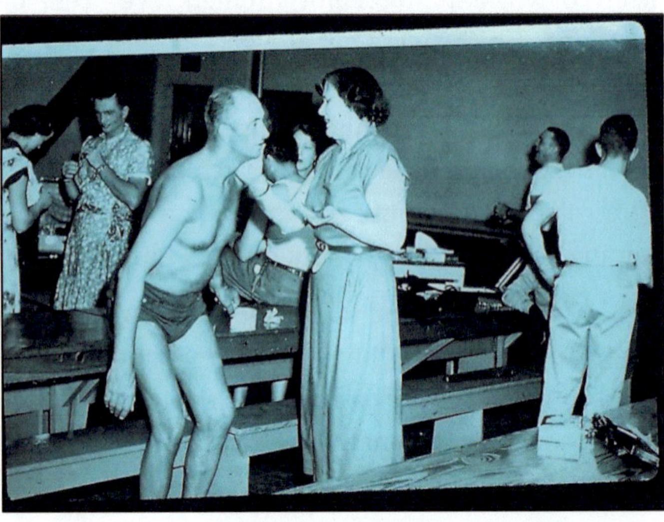

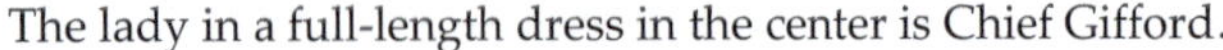

The lady in a full-length dress in the center is Chief Gifford.

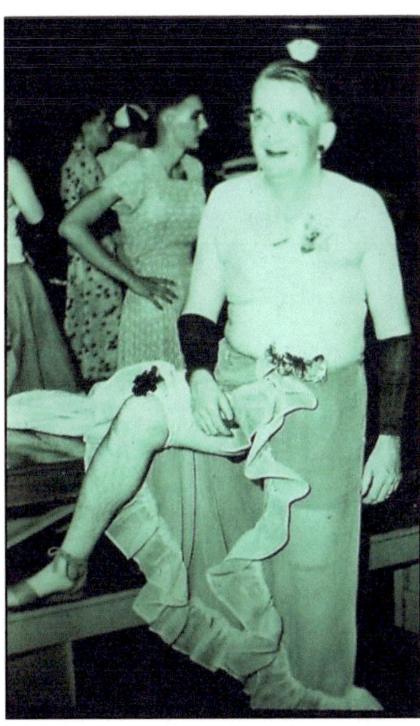

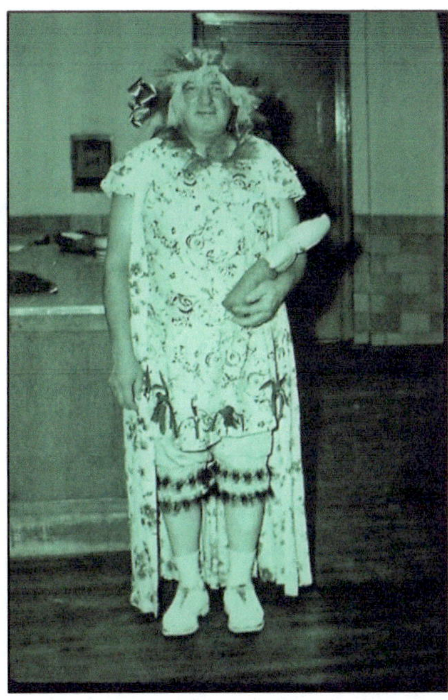

Red Neapolitan

The shows were often held in the gymnasium and the small auditorium of the high school. The cast included about a dozen Boardman firefighters. Attendance was considered good at around 200 people per show. Occasionally, shows would be put on in collaboration with other fire departments, and the net profits were shared.

✠ *Fire Trucks* ✠

The following is the inventory of all of the fire apparatus used by Boardman Fire Department.

> Gifford organized the Boardman volunteer fire fighters who operated from an old garage, using a pushcart as their only equipment.

Initially, the fire department's only equipment was a trailer to which two 40-gallon water tanks were attached. They added a gasoline powered water pump and some rubber hose to the outfit. On the hose was a straight tip brass nozzle. It was reported that the fire wagon was stored in a spare garage at the Smith Dairy located on Southern Boulevard before the small fire station was built. Chief Gifford would take his pickup truck over to the garage at the time of a fire call, hook up the fire wagon and haul it to the fire scene. Even after the Township purchased a real fire truck, the fire wagon was still used. The wagon, when pulled by a car, could only achieve a top speed of about 25 miles per hour. Otter Elser was assigned to get the trailer one day. After hooking up the wagon, he reached the scene of the fire 25 minutes later even though the fire was only four miles from the garage!

The Boardman Fire Department chemical cart looked like this.

There seem to be several versions of this first "fire truck." This one appears in a Vindicator article in 1966 announcing Chief Gifford's retirement from Austintown. He tells this story; the first truck was ordered by Trustees Charles Geiger, Olin Stafford, and Samuel McClurg. The firemen eagerly waited for its arrival. Everyone was acutely disappointed, including Gifford, to find they owned a two-wheeled cart with two 40-gallon soda acid chemical tanks. Gifford related that after the first fire in which it was used, the men wheeled the apparatus to Geiger's front yard and parked it there. The 1923 Model T was ordered shortly afterward.

On November 13, 1923, Boardman Township Trustee William Geiger signed a Bill of Sale for a Ford truck with a fire truck body from the Ford Motor Company for $641 just weeks after the decision was made to officially form Boardman Fire Department.

Harold Slagle: "The first fire truck was on an old Model T Ford and there was room for a couple to sit in the front with the driver and there was a step on the back where people could stand. It didn't go very fast and if it hit a bump, your feet bounced you off the back step and you were running behind and you had to jump back on."

BILL OF SALE, IN DUPLICATE
(MOTOR VEHICLE)

KNOW ALL MEN BY THESE PRESENTS, That Wm Geiger

Residence, No. .... *Street, City of* Mt. Springhill *Ohio,*

the Grantor..., for the consideration of Six hundred & Seventy One

*Dollars ($*671.00*), paid by* Bordman twp.

Street and No. .... *City of* ~~Bordman~~ Colan *Ohio,*
the Grantee..., the receipt of which is hereby acknowledged, do..... hereby grant, bargain, sell, transfer, and deliver unto the Grantee... the following described motor vehicle:

Manufacturer or Maker Ford Motor Co. ;

engine or motor number 8270150 *; other numbers* .... ;

horse power 22½ *; description of body* Fire truck

.... ;

other marks of identification ....

(If an imported vehicle, the following must be filled in)

Importer .... ;

City and Country of Manufacturer ....

Port of Exportation .... *Port of Importation* ....

Original purchaser ....

To have and to hold the same unto the said Grantee... and... h..... executors, administrators, and assigns, forever.

And the said Grantor... hereby covenant... to and with the said Grantee... that said Grantor... ...... the lawful owner..... of the above described motor vehicle; that the same is free from all incumbrances whatsoever; except ....

.... ;

that said Grantor... ha..... good right to sell the same as aforesaid; and that said Grantor... will warrant and defend the same against all lawful claims and demands whatsoever, except ....

IN WITNESS WHEREOF, the said Wm Geiger

*ha*s *hereunto set* his *hand this* 13 *day of* Nov. 1923

Witnessed by

Thomas Greer — Wm Geiger

J. F. Kauffman

OATH

State of Ohio, Mahoning County, ss.:

Wm Geiger

*being duly sworn say*s *that the statements in the foregoing Bill of Sale are true and correct as* ... he... *verily believe*s

Wm Geiger

Sworn to before me and signed in my presence this 13 *day of* Nov. 1923

Fred Gelger

Notary Public

Mahoning *County, Ohio.*

Merle Gifford's granddaughters, Debby Campbell, and Judy Parsons, informed me that they had their grandfather's scrapbook. Shortly afterward, I received a packet in the mail. Inside were three 3" X 5" black and white photos that had not been seen by anyone in the modern times of the fire department. In fact, no one knew what the first fire truck looked like. The pictures revealed to us both the first and second trucks owned by the fire department. The smaller truck on the right is the first fire truck, a 1923 Model T Ford. The larger of the trucks is a 1927 Model A Ford. In this first picture, the trucks are in front of the first brick and mortar station at 136 Boardman Poland Road. It was only a single bay. The second bay was later added to the right side.

Merle Gifford's grocery store is the building on the right. Examine the trucks all over to see the various items of equipment they carried. The bell on the smaller truck is in the possession of Gifford's granddaughters.

Look closely on the right hand side of the second picture for the gas pumps on the right side of the grocery store.

Barney Davison said, "Swede Nordquist talked about the department having a Model T chemical wagon. Some chemical wagons had a 60-gallon drum of water that could be used on the spot without the need for a pump. The water was expelled by carbon dioxide gas created by the action of sulphuric acid with a bicarbonate solution. The result was a reasonably powerful jet of water which was an effective front line of attack until the heavier water lines could be brought in to use from the trucks with fire pumps. Once the chemical tank was activated, it could not be turned off. It had to completely empty itself. If only a little water was needed, the rest was wasted and there was none left in the event of another outbreak at a separate place in the building. One solution was to have several tanks on the truck that could be activated separately."

Swede told Davison, "One of the tanks was under the driver's seat. You had to make sure that the hose line was out and ready to go and the tank valves were open when you mixed the chemical and activated the chemical reaction or you would blow the truck up. Swede complained that Gifford always wanted the old fenders of the Model T chemical wagon to shine; he wanted them perfect. The fenders were old and pitted but Swede had to shine them to perfection for the Chief." Stories have been told that the truck had not been delivered painted red so the firemen, with the help of residents of the community, painted it red.

9/14/1927-A Seagrave fire truck was bought in Columbus Ohio. It was capable of pumping 500 gallons of water per minute.

3/26/1928 Trustees made a motion to trade the present Ford Truck for a 1928 model roadster.

10/16/1929- The Trustees traded the small fire truck for a Ford Roadster to be used by the Fire Chief.

11/6/1929- A new Ford Roadster was delivered.

In February of 1939, the roadster, having served its purpose, was sold to Clarence Nordquist for $35.00.

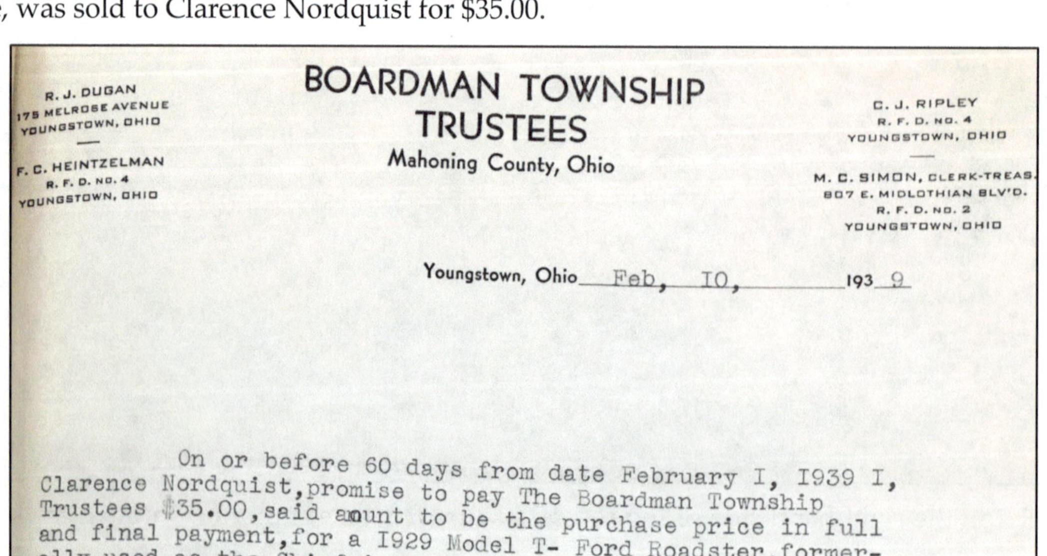

R. J. DUGAN
175 MELROSE AVENUE
YOUNGSTOWN, OHIO

F. C. HEINTZELMAN
R. F. D. NO. 4
YOUNGSTOWN, OHIO

BOARDMAN TOWNSHIP
TRUSTEES
Mahoning County, Ohio

C. J. RIPLEY
R. F. D. NO. 4
YOUNGSTOWN, OHIO

M. C. SIMON, CLERK-TREAS.
807 E. MIDLOTHIAN BLV'D.
R. F. D. NO. 2
YOUNGSTOWN, OHIO

Youngstown, Ohio Feb, IO, 1939

On or before 60 days from date February I, 1939 I, Clarence Nordquist,promise to pay The Boardman Township Trustees $35.00,said amunt to be the purchase price in full and final payment,for a I929 Model T- Ford Roadster,formerally used as the Chiefs' car by the Boardman Fire Dept.

3/5/1930- Trustees Meeting Minutes: Motion to pay the Seagrave Corporation for repairs to a fire truck $1.40.

According to an article written in 1959- In 1934, a Ford 800-gallon pumper was added which was put together by our own men. They built their own truck.

12/5/1934- Trustee Meeting Minutes: Motion to send the fire truck to Columbus, Ohio, to the Seagrave Corporation Factory for a general overhaul, and that we hire Howard Kyle to take the fire truck down and stay and bring the same back. Note- Kyle was paid $18.05.

1935- The fire department owns a 1935 Ford Seagrave V8 fire truck with a Barton-American front mount pump.

This truck, which can be seen on the far left hand side of page 24, has been a mystery to me. I had originally felt that it fit the descriptions in meeting minutes but I was never sure. I reached out to an antique fire truck association and presented them with this picture. Within hours several had identified it as a 1935 Ford Seagrave V8 truck. Others felt it was a mid-thirties Ford truck. An internet search of Ford V8 trucks from 1933 to 1938 zeroed in on the 1935 Ford. I am convinced this is the 1935 model. The following pictures should satisfy most anyone that this is the 1935 model but also provide us with our first good look at all sides of one of our oldest trucks.

Pictured in front are Sig Nordquist, James Austin, and Kermit Carlson. In the rear is Don Davis.

MBA
FIRE DEPT

MBA
FIRE DEPT.

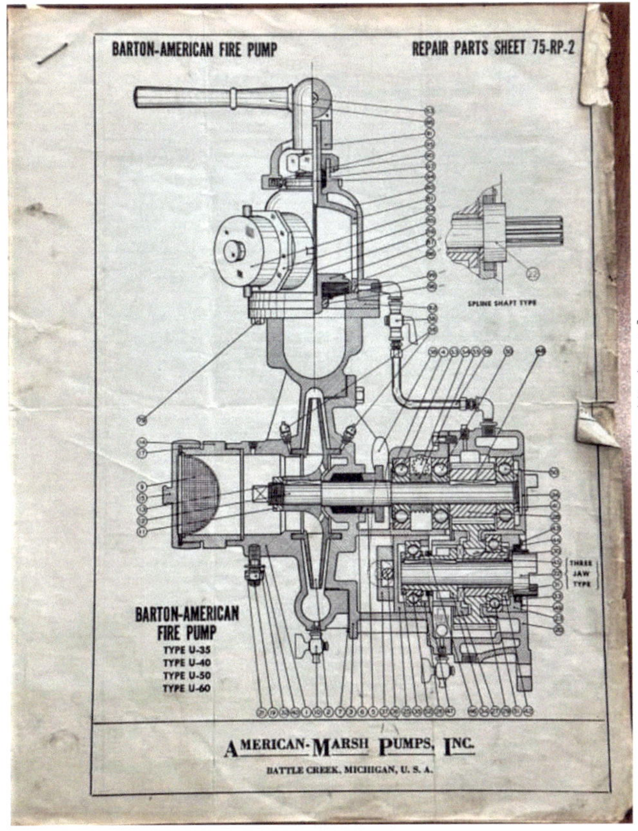

The schematic for the Barton-American front mounted pump for the 1935 Ford Seagrave. .

5/6/1936- The new fire truck is now equipped with a new, modern pump. From the Journal on the same date: Hose is to be purchased when the two new pieces of apparatus are equipped. An inventory of apparatus belonging to the fire department in 1942 indicates that in 1936 they purchased an "assembled Ford Fire Truck." I take this to mean they purchased a truck that was sold to Boardman as a complete fire truck. In April of 1953, this truck was auctioned for $240.

The 1942 inventory also showed that in 1936 the department owned a 1936 car. This was likely for the Fire Chief.

March 1937- The fire department got a new truck to be used when water was not available on the north end. It has a 500-gallon tank. This truck was designated as Truck 202.

7/21/1037- Trustees opened bids on a new fire truck.

When asked how the 200 series numbers were chosen for the fire trucks, Barney Davison said, "There was a time that a new truck was generally assigned to work out of the Number 2 Station, therefore it picked up 200 designations: 201, 202, 203, etc."

Later, in the nineties, the numbering system was changed, to facilitate working with other departments during mutual aid. Many departments had designated their pumper trucks Engine 1 and Engine 2 and so on. Everybody had an Engine 1 and a Ladder 1. So, to avoid confusion, when working together, the Chiefs got together and assigned each department a number series. Boardman was assigned the 700 series. Stations became Station 71, 73, and 74. Trucks became Engine 71, Squad 71, and Ladder 71. The Fire Chief became Fire 70.

This 1937 Seagrave Sedan is the first enclosed fire truck in the State of Ohio. Outside of the truck is Chief Gifford, R. A. Smith President of the Volunteer Fire Department, R. J. Dugan Trustee, C. J. Ripley Trustee, F. C. Heintzelman Trustee, and K. E. Heintzelman firefighter. Chief Gifford is in the lower oval. The Sedan cost the township $10,000. The truck could carry eight men and delivered 750 GPM from draft. This was purchased to help reduce the fire insurance ratings.

Boardman Tries Out New High-Speed Fire Equip...

MAR., 1953

PAGE FOUR — THE BOARDMAN NEWS —

"GRASS FIRES ARE COSTLY in more ways than one," said Merle W. Gifford, Boardman's fire chief, following Thursday's fire-truck auto collision at the intersection of Routes 224 and 7—Boardman Center. The truck, traveling west on 224 enroute to a grass fire west of Glenwood Ave. extension, was struck by a car driven by James Hill of Morgantown, W. Va., traveling north on Route 7. No one was injured. Gil Simons was driving the fire truck.

This picture was taken in front of Number 2 Station on Market Street and shows the Chief's car which was purchased in 1927.

The Trustees bought the Seagrave fire truck in 1937. The covered Seagrave was affectionately called Nellie Bell by the firefighters who used her. The designation was Truck 202. Firefighters could enter the enclosed section. The center was open and there were bench seats on both sides. Underneath one seat was a ladder and under the other seat was fire hose. It had a 500-gallon tank. It was bought pre-owned by Cleveland Fire Department. Bill Bush said, "This truck was nasty to drive. It did not have power steering."

After sitting behind Station 3, for years rusting, the 1937 Seagrave Sedan was sold at auction for $240 on April 23, 1953.

Boardman Volunteer Fire Department   Decoration Day

Don Davis   M. Alexander   1927 Seagrave   D. Hendeman

Sig Nordquist James Austin Kermit Carlson John L. deSaulles Larry Nordquist Homer Hall Wm. Mcintosh

May 30, 1939 **'Our First Uniforms'**

Fred LaBelle Jr. 1937 Seagrave J. D. Smith

Clay Nordquist P. Bender A. Zima Al Hanna J. C. Heintzelman Howard Jessop Merle Gifford Chief

9/5/1940- Trustees Meeting Minutes:

MINUTES OF MEETING HELD SEPT. 5, I940.
At Twelve Noon.

At an adjourned meeting of the Trustees of Boardman Township, Mahonong County, Ohio,held on the above date, Mr. J. Donald Smith, Mr. F. C. Heintzelman and Mr. C. J. Ripley being present, the following business was transacted.

At this time sealed bids were received and opened, from the following Companies:

Seagrave Corporation, Columbus, Ohio	$I3,950.00 Net
American LaFrance Foamite Corp. Pitts.Pa.	I2,394.00 5%
Mack Manufacturing Corp.	I3,5I8.00 Net
Buffalo Fire Appliance Corp.Buffalo, N. Y.	I2,788.27 5%

3/6/1941- Trustees Meeting Minutes: Motion made to accept and pay $13,518 for the Mack Fire Truck to Mack Truck Inc. Motion passed by Heintzelman, Smith, and Ripley.

MINUTES OF MEETING HELD MARCH 6, I94I.

At a regular meeting of the Trustees of Boardman Township, Mahoning County, Ohio, held on the above date, Mr. C. J. Ripley Mr. J. Donald Smith and Mr. F. C. Heintzelman were present . The minutes of Feb. 6, I94I, were read and approved and the following business was transacted.

Moved by Mr. Heintzelman that we accept and pay for the Mack Fire Truck$I3,5I8.00 as per our contract and $200.00 for air brakes as per our contract, and $30.00 for an extra suction hose trough.
Second by Mr. Smith.
Mr. Heintzelman, Yes. Mr. Smith, Yes. Mr. Ripley, Yes.

Moved by Mr. Heintzelman that we purchase the necessary miscellaneous equipment from the Seagrave Corp.

Proud? You Betcha! For Boardman Fire Truck Is "Latest"

Proud as a boy with a new toy are these Boardmen firemen as they pose beside the latest piece of apparatus purchased by the department—a $13,700 fire truck complete with the latest equipment, and paid for without a loan or a bond issue. The new squad car, accepted by the department last week, pumps 1,154 gallons of water a minute; has a 200-gallon booster tank; two 500-watt floodlights and one 250-watt searchlight mounted behind the cab. Fire Chief Merrill W. Gifford, by the cab door, is proud of the truck's air brakes, and says the Boardman truck is the only truck outside of New York fire department that has air brakes. The truck replaces a 15-year-old Seagrave pumper. Other firemen in the picture are A. G. Hanna, in black coat, and Roy Parker, assistant chief.

The fire department purchased a 1941 Mack Fire Truck designated as Truck 203. As WWII started in 1941, certain metals were being restricted for use in the war effort. Thus, the Mack was the last fire track made with chrome trim. The Mack had a 750 GPM pump and a 300-gallon tank. As with other older trucks, this truck had no power steering and was very hard to drive. In 1972, the Mack was a backup truck. If I drove this truck for any length of time, my leg would tremble with fatigue because the clutch was so stiff. Barney Davison said, "Both the International and the Mack trucks had stiff clutches. The steering on the Mack was also difficult to handle until the department added air assist to make the steering easier."

The 1941 Mack in one of many parades.

1/26/1942- Trustees Meeting Minutes: A motion is made to purchase a Buckeye Pontiac emergency car. Also, to purchase one model C-5 siren from Harry Sutphen at $100.

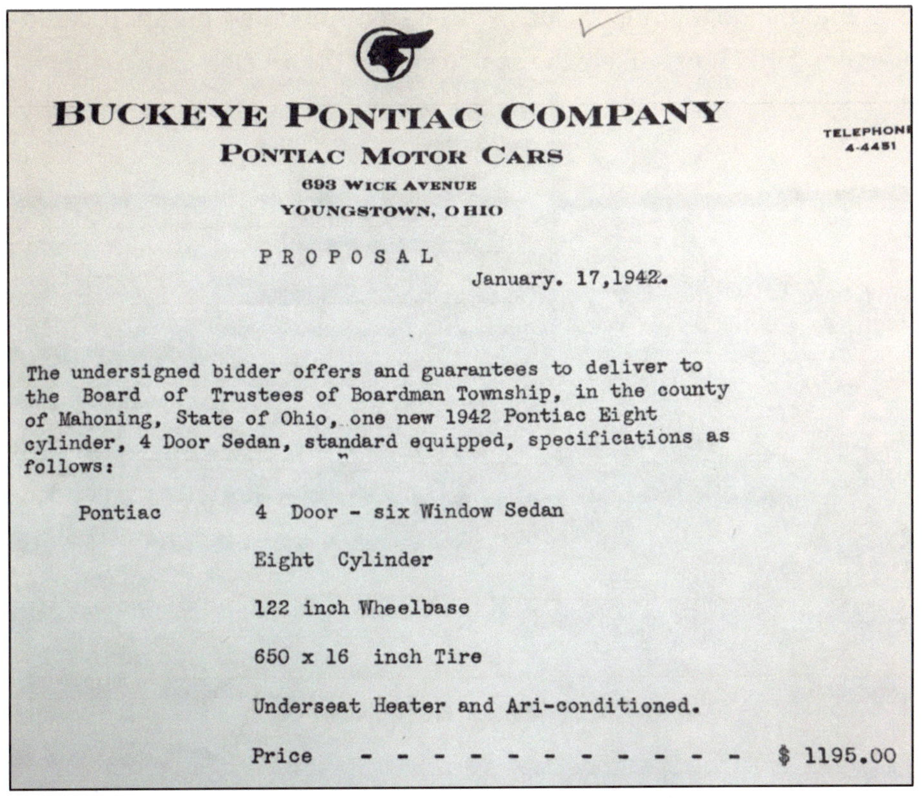

BUCKEYE PONTIAC COMPANY
PONTIAC MOTOR CARS
693 WICK AVENUE
YOUNGSTOWN, OHIO

TELEPHONE
4-4451

PROPOSAL

January. 17,1942.

The undersigned bidder offers and guarantees to deliver to the Board of Trustees of Boardman Township, in the county of Mahoning, State of Ohio, one new 1942 Pontiac Eight cylinder, 4 Door Sedan, standard equipped, specifications as follows:

Pontiac — 4 Door - six Window Sedan

Eight Cylinder

122 inch Wheelbase

650 x 16 inch Tire

Underseat Heater and Ari-conditioned.

Price - - - - - - - - - - - - - $ 1195.00

A 1942 Pontiac similar to the one Boardman owned.

Federal C-5 Siren

An article written in 1959 states: In 1947, a 500-gallon International tanker was also added to the growing equipment of the department. Truck Number 5 was also called 205.

There was a 1949 International pumper truck with a front-mounted pump. It could pump 750 GPM and had an 800-gallon tank. It was likely the same truck in the article.

It was later sold to Camp Fitch for campfire protection.

In 1953, Boardman was awarded $6,625 from the Federal Civil Defense Administration for financial assistance to purchase a fire truck. The truck was a GMC, purchased from Sutphen and designated as Truck 204. The CD logo was required to be on the doors of the truck. Along with the truck came the first Chemox air packs that the department had ever seen. After the war, the government wanted to protect certain assets. The steel mills in Youngstown were considered one of the nation's assets. Therefore the U.S. Government wanted to provide the communities near the mills with additional fire apparatus.

Truck 201 was a 1952 Seagrave pumper.

Vic Sedlako & JB deSaulles

(L-R) FF Paul McAllister A/C Larry (Swede) Nordquist Jr FF Dave Carlson

When Bill Bush was interviewed for a full-time job with the department by the Trustees, Faye Heintzelman, Al Hannah, and Bill Mansell, Heintzelman asked Bush how he liked the new truck. Bush responded that he did not know yet as it was new. He said, "Ask me in 6 months." Heintzelman did ask him again in 6 months and Bush, one to always speak his mind said, " I don't like it." The truck had been ordered with an aluminum ladder but arrived with a wooden ladder painted aluminum color. On the first fire that called for a ladder to be placed on a building, it broke in half when a firefighter started to climb it. After that, a real aluminum ladder was ordered from Sutphen.

Over the years, Boardman Fire Department bought several Ford trucks and then bought three Seagrave trucks from a Columbus, Ohio dealer. There was an International, a GMC, and a Mack. Then in 1963, Boardman bought its first Sutphen made pumper truck. In 1966, bought its first aerial ladder truck from Sutphen. As of the summer of 2019, Sutphen Corporation had sold Boardman 15 fire apparatus. Sutphen trucks met the needs of Boardman Fire Department over the years with quality trucks at a competitive price. The Sutphen Company began in 1890 when they began to sell fire equipment and fire trucks made by other manufacturers such as GMC and Peter Pirsch. In 1955, they began to manufacture fire trucks and sold them under their own name.

Dan Herb from the Sutphen Corporation in Columbus Ohio sold fire trucks to Boardman for as long as I can remember. He was not just a salesman, he knew the trucks, and he knew the dynamics and function of all of the components of the truck. Not only did he sell, but he was also an educator. He was able to train the buyer on the operation of every piece of equipment that he sold. His knowledge did not stop with fire trucks but extended into other equipment that Sutphen sold. In the early 1970s, the fire department bought its first vehicle rescue tools, The Hurst Rescue Tools! Dan Herb came to Boardman and put on a hands-on demonstration of the tools on a junk car. He did it carefully enough that we were able to record the training session and use it as an educational tool for other firefighters.

In 1959, Smith Dairy donated a 1950 Chevrolet panel truck for use by the Junior Firefighters. The Trustees, at a meeting, voted to accept the truck and provide insurance for it.

The truck on the left is from a picture outside of the Smith Dairy business at Southern Boulevard and Route 224.
The truck on the left is the same model dairy truck so we can see what the truck looked like.

There was a time when our department needed a new rescue truck. After making our choice, we had the opportunity to perform a final inspection of the truck at the manufacturing plant in Florida. Assistant Chief Joe Romeo and I made the trip down and were met by our sales representative. We checked into our ocean-front hotel. Late in the day, Joe and I were going to enjoy some beach time and we were heading to the shoreline when we heard a fuss being made by a group of people. As it turned out, an elderly man had just been pulled out of the water and was not breathing. Romeo and I immediately began the CPR/ rescue breathing process and continued until the local EMS arrived. Our efforts were unfortunately unsuccessful. The next day we were informed that the son of the man who we had tried to resuscitate wanted to buy us dinner to express his gratitude for our attempt to save his father's life.

This Chief's car, a Plymouth, was purchased in 1957.

Fire Chief Gifford To Attend Conclave

Boardman Fire Chief Merle W. Gifford will attend the 84th annual convention of the International Association of Fire Chiefs the week of Sept. 8. The convention will be held this year in New Orleans.

Gifford, a past president of the Great Lakes Division of that association, will be attending his 18th meeting of the association. Gifford has been chief of the local department for better than 30 years.

Keeping Up-to-Date

BOARDMAN'S FIRE DEPARTMENT has taken another step to keep it o[illegible] of the best in the country, adding a new fire chief's car to the five new truc[illegible] purchased recently by the township. Shown here (inset) is Chief Gifford glo[illegible]ing proudly at the new station wagon.

A display of fire apparatus in the sixties.

The manufacturer of the truck on the right was Peter Pirsch. It was purchased in 1961. When I joined the department, I was assigned to Station Number 4 to work on A-Shift with Wayne Ewing. This is the first truck that I learned to drive and pump.

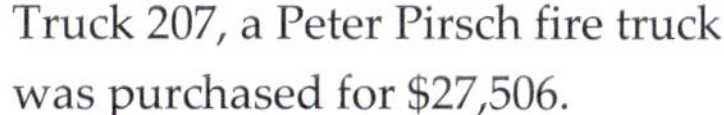

Truck 207, a Peter Pirsch fire truck was purchased for $27,506.

"BIG RED" is the unofficial name of the brand-new fire engine which has just been delivered and is now housed at Boardman's modern station at Lockwood Blvd. and Shields Road. In the photo at the left, Fire Chief Wayne Ewing proudly gives it a going over.

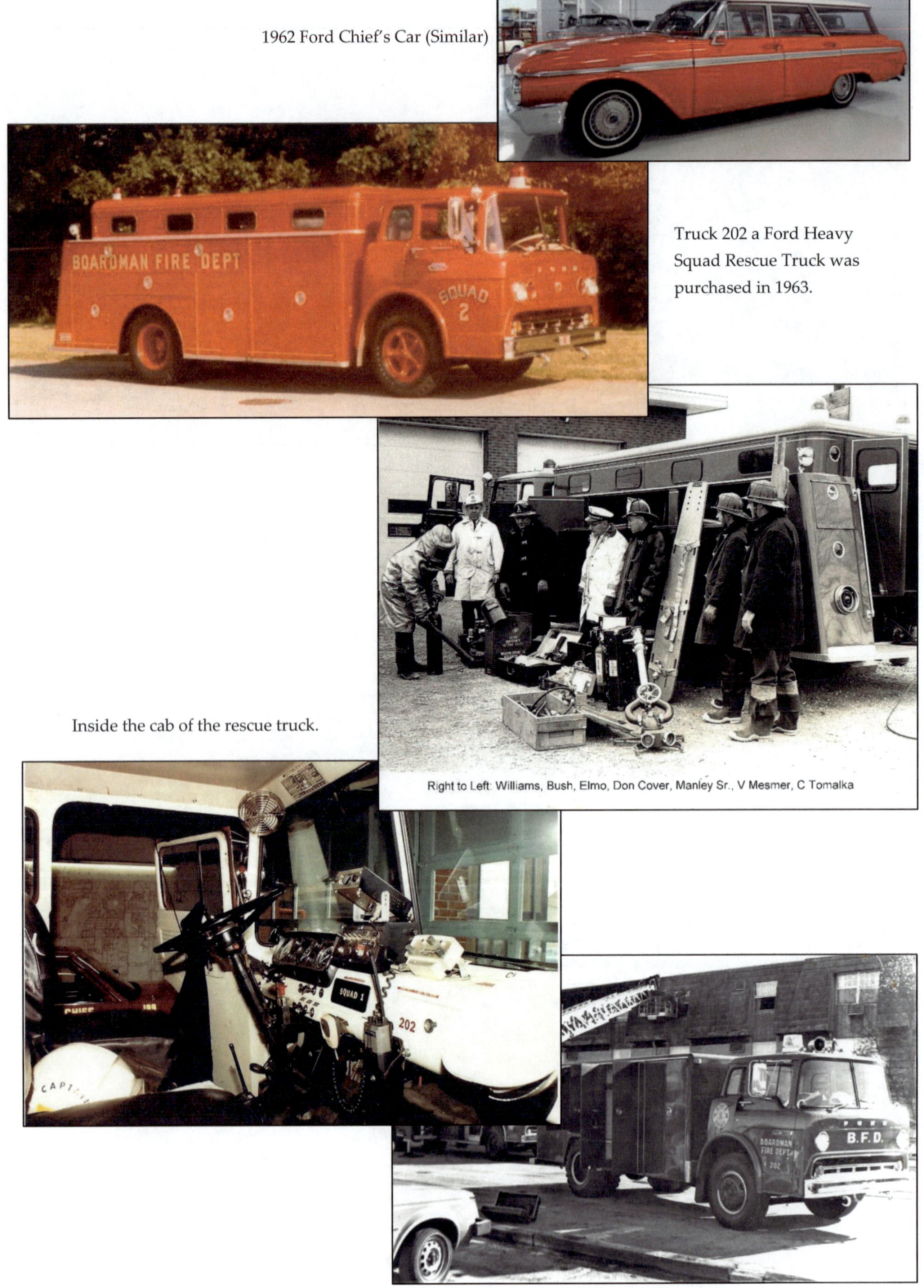

1962 Ford Chief's Car (Similar)

Truck 202 a Ford Heavy Squad Rescue Truck was purchased in 1963.

Right to Left: Williams, Bush, Elmo, Don Cover, Manley Sr., V Mesmer, C Tomalka

Inside the cab of the rescue truck.

Chief's Car 199 was a 1968 Pontiac Station Wagon.

Truck 208, a 90′ aerial platform, was purchased in 1966.

Truck 204 was purchased in 1971.

Truck 204 undergoing a pump test using a creek in Mill Creek Park to draft water.

1973 Pontiac Chief's Car (Similar)

Truck 201 was purchased in 1973 from the Sutphen Corporation. It had a Ford turbine engine. It was the first turbine engine fire truck ever sold. This was a radical move for the normally conservative Fire Chief. Chief Cover and the Trustees took a chance on the new approach to fire truck engines. But this experiment was plagued from the beginning. The electronics of the radio system interfered with the computer that controlled the engine. The fire truck engine would suddenly quit on route to an emergency. Despite efforts to correct the problem, it could not be resolved. In less than a year, Ford recalled the engine and replaced the turbine engine with a more conventional diesel engine.

Truck 201, in Columbus, during its pump certification test.

Kenneth F. Smith
General Sales and Marketing Manager

Industrial Engine and Turbine Division
Ford Motor Company
P.O. Box 1796
Dearborn, Michigan

July 10, 1973

Mr. Don Cover
Fire Chief
Boardman Township
Youngstown, Ohio

Dear Mr. Cover:

Ford Motor Company has decided to discontinue marketing the 3600 and 4200 models of its 707 Series gas turbine engines. Therefore, the Industrial Engine and Turbine Division is recalling these series turbine engines currently in customer hands and making provisions for repowering with appropriate diesel power.

Ford will pay for all costs directly associated with the removal of the turbines and installation of diesel power. Ford will also reimburse you for any price difference between the turbines and the diesels we install. You will be contacted by a Ford representative to make specific arrangements for the repowering, including timing. Since it is not planned to continue field service support indefinitely, we shall endeavor to complete your engine changeover by year end. Meanwhile, normal field service will continue.

Ford regrets having to take this action. We believe, however, this action is in your best interest, because the current 707 Series turbine has not demonstrated the durability we believe customers expect from Ford products. Ford is continuing its turbine development program and presently is concentrating all its efforts on a "second generation" gas turbine designated the 710. Market availability of this engine is projected for the late 1970's or the 1980's.

If you have any questions regarding the contents of this letter, please direct them to Mr. B. K. Arbuckle, On Highway Sales Manager, (313) 323-4420.

Sincerely,

K. F. Smith

cc: Mr. Tom Sutphen, Sutphen Fire Equipment
Mr. J. R. Ford, Graham Ford

This vehicle was purchased for use by the Fire Prevention Officer. Car 197 was a 1975 Chevrolet El Camino, similar to the one pictured here. The bed could be loaded with hose, air packs, and other equipment that needed put back in service after a fire.

Truck 205 was purchased in 1976 from Sutphen Corporation for $60,000. It had a 1250-gallon pump and a 500-gallon tank. It was traded for a new truck in 1999.

In 1979, the department purchased a Ford Super Vac Heavy Rescue Truck similar to this vehicle. The old Squad 202 was traded in for the new truck which also took the number 202.

In 1982, the department purchased two Ford LTDs similar to this vehicle. One was used by the Fire Chief and the other by the Fire Prevention Officer.

Truck 206 was purchased in 1983 from Sutphen. Its designation was later changed to 706. This is the first truck purchased that had an automatic transmission. The truck was purchased for $134,000. The truck had a 1250-gallon pump with a 500-gallon water tank.

Standing next to 206 are Gary Houser, Mike Grossman, and Steve Hierro. Kneeling are Jim Dorman, Don Mauch, and Ed Gibson.

In April 2009, Truck 706 was sold at auction for $2,475.

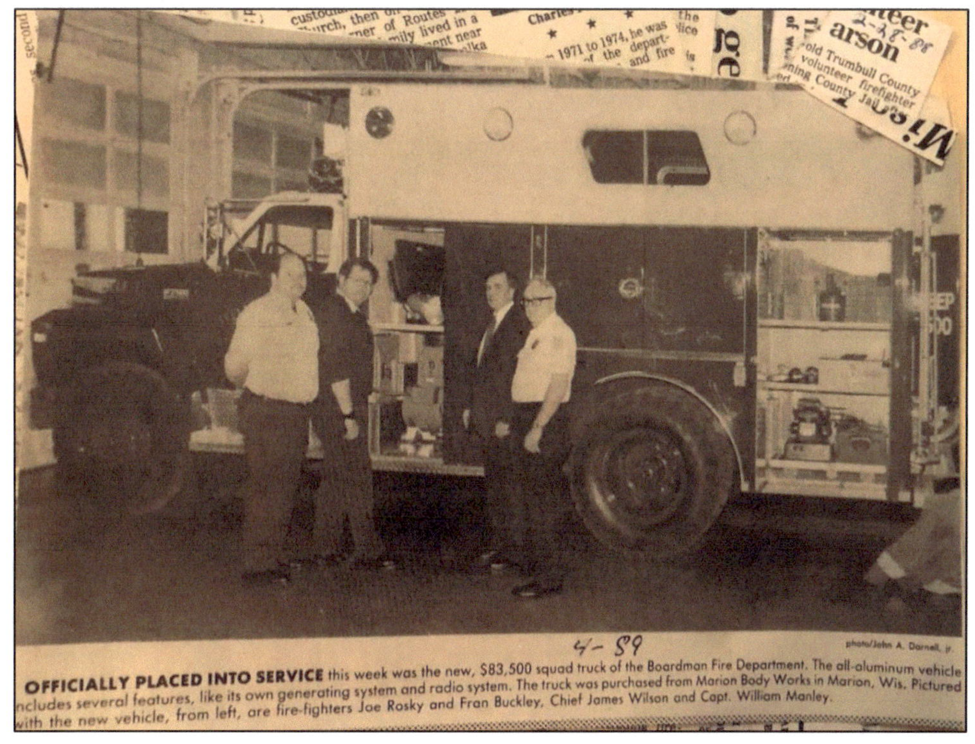

4-89

photo/John A. Darnell, Jr.

OFFICIALLY PLACED INTO SERVICE this week was the new, $83,500 squad truck of the Boardman Fire Department. The all-aluminum vehicle includes several features, like its own generating system and radio system. The truck was purchased from Marion Body Works in Marion, Wis. Pictured with the new vehicle, from left, are fire-fighters Joe Rosky and Fran Buckley, Chief James Wilson and Capt. William Manley.

A new rescue truck, designated as Rescue 1, was purchased in 1989 from Marion Body Works. It was purchased for $87,000. With the purchase of this truck, Boardman Fire Department changed the mission of rescue squads from heavy rescue to a quick response unit oriented toward emergency medical care. Vehicle rescue tools would soon be purchased for each front line pumper truck as well as the aerial truck. There was no longer a need to have a large, centralized rescue vehicle.

In 1991, the department replaced its first aerial platform ladder truck with this purchase from the Sutphen Corporation. This truck was designated Truck 208 and was later changed to Truck 709. The truck was diesel powered and had a 95′ tower.

1992 GMC Safari Van 197. This vehicle was assigned to the Fire Investigation Unit with appropriate equipment to investigate fires.

1992 Ford Crown Victoria Chief's car was designated Car 199. Later this vehicle was transferred to the Fire Prevention Bureau.

1995 A Sutphen pumper body was placed on a Spartan chassis with a Spartan cab. The designation was originally Engine One, then 207, then 707. This was purchased as a low cost alternative to a standard pumper truck. However, it was found to be underpowered and had a lighter than the accustomed frame and an inadequate electrical system. It was a constant source of problems for the vehicle mechanics.

1997 A Sutphen Pumper Truck was designated as 201 and was later changed to 701.

1998 A Ford Crown Victoria was designated as Car 199 and was later changed to 799. Used by the Fire Chief.

1999 A Sutphen Pumper Truck was designated as 205 and was later changed to 705.

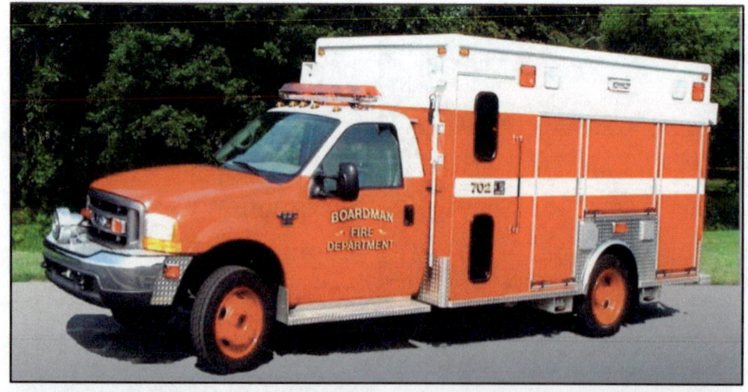

2000 An EVI Ford F-550 Light Duty Rescue Truck that was designated as Truck 702.

2000 A Ford Taurus designated as Car 796 was assigned to the Fire Prevention Office as an inspection vehicle.

2001 A Ford Excursion designated Car 795 was assigned to the Assistant Chief on duty for use as a Command Vehicle.

2003 A Ford Expedition designated Car 794 was assigned to Fire Prevention.

2004 A Ford Crown Victoria designated Car 799 was assigned to the Fire Chief.

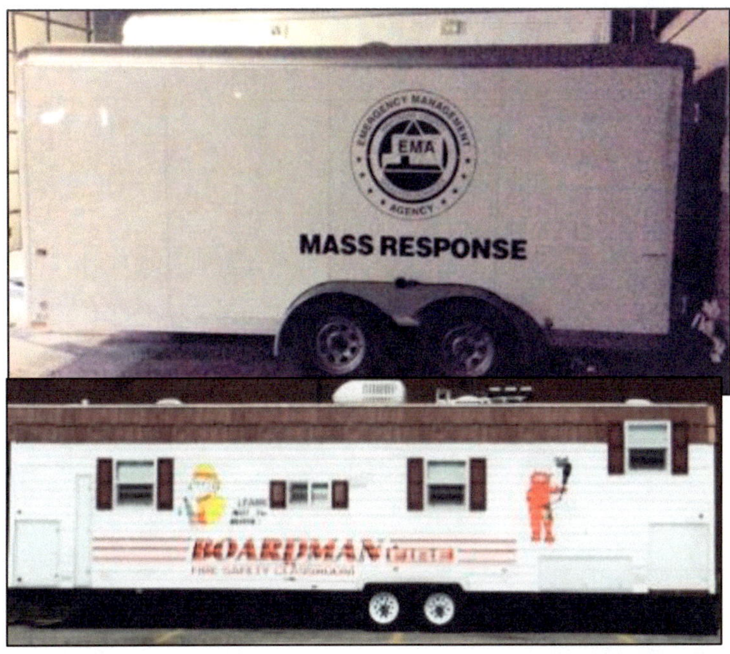

2004 A Mass Casualty Response trailer was placed in the custody of Boardman Fire Department by The Mahoning County Emergency Management Agency. This vehicle was stocked with supplies that would be needed if an incident occurred with many injuries.

2005 A Mobile Fire Safety Classroom trailer was purchased with the assistance of a Federal Grant.

2004 A Dodge ¾ ton utility truck designated Truck 793 was assigned to the Fire Prevention Office for use with inspections and to tow the Mobile Fire Safety Trailer.

2004 A Sutphen Quint pumper truck with a 60′ ladder. This truck was designated Truck 704.

2006 A GMC Safari Van was assigned to the Fire Investigation Unit replacing the original vehicle. The van was designated 797.

2007 A Sutphen Pumper was designated Truck 702.

2010 A Hummer was transferred from the police department to the fire department. It was an acquisition from a drug bust. Used as an off-road brush fire truck.

2012 Ford Expedition Car 799 was assigned for use by the Fire Chief.

2012 Ford Interceptor Car 792 was used by the Fire Prevention Bureau.

2012 E-One 102′ Ladder was designated as L-74 and 708.

2013 Ford Expedition designated as 795 and used as the Command Vehicle by the Assistant Chief.

2016 Sutphen Pumper designated as E-73 and 705.

2017 Ford Interceptor designated as 794. This vehicle was assigned to the Fire Prevention Bureau.

In 2020, this 1992 E-One 95′ Aerial Platform truck was purchased from Canfield-Cardinal Joint Fire District for $30,000 as a backup to Ladder 74 which was having recurring mechanical problems. This truck was designated as T-71 and 706.

2022 Chevrolet Silverado designated as 799 and assigned to the Fire Chief. The special markings indicate the Chief's vehicle and make it stand out for easy recognition at an emergency.

✠ Fire Stations ✠

Most Boardman firefighters consider 136 Boardman Poland Road to be the location of our first fire station This has turned out not to be the case. While it is true that this is the location of the first full-scale building used to house fire trucks and provide a meeting location and a place to sleep for the full-time firefighters, it was not the first building erected to house fire equipment. The reality is that our first fire station was located 250 yards east of the 136 Boardman Poland Road fire station and on the other side of the road at 321 Boardman Poland Road. In an interview, Chief Gifford states, "The fire department originated on September 10, 1923, in front of the Boardman Supply office." Chief Cover said, "They first set up on the corner of Southern Boulevard and Route 224. There was a little grocery store there that Gifford ran at the time. They had a shed by the grocery store and that's where they put their first piece of equipment."

The First Fire Station was located at 321 Boardman Poland Road.

What led to the artist's rendering of our first fire station?

The scene depicted in this drawing was produced after I read the transcripts of many people interviewed for another book on the history of Boardman. Residents, many born in the early 1900s, participated in the interview process. After reading accounts of that first fire station, I had a picture in my mind of what the grocery store and first fire station may have looked like. I created a rough drawing of what I thought the scene may have looked like and then asked Penny Badolato, my son-in-law's mother if she could sketch the scene. She is an accomplished artist. She agreed and produced this picture. She spent time researching the construction of grocery stores and garages from the early 1920s to give her drawing a feeling of structures in 1923. She then used her talents to bring all of this information together on paper. I wanted to give the reader a good idea of what may have been on the corner of Route 224 and Southern Boulevard based on the eyewitness descriptions, some research, and an educated guess or two. Her drawing perfectly fit what I had imagined sitting on that corner with people stopping in for gas or groceries and the tiny fire truck racing out of the garage from time to time to keep a home from burning to the ground. Here are some of the comments that help give life to the picture of our first fire station.

On the canvas awning over the storefront, next to 136 Boardman Poland Road, was printed the store name: Gifford and Laucks Grocery. This was Gifford and Laucks', second grocery store. So, I assumed that the first store also had the same signage.

Bob Davis: "The station was a single-car garage almost like a shed. The siren was on a pole next to the garage. A button, on the pole, was pushed to activate the siren (to blow the whistle)."

The Mahoning Dispatch May 23, 1923: Merle Gifford and C. E. Laucks bought a gas station and store from the Heintzelman Brothers. This building was located east of the Southern Boulevard railroad tracks on Boardman Poland Road.

An article written in 1958: The very first fire station was a garage, 14 by 20 feet, heated by oil and located about where the Boardman Supply Company is now located.

Mrs. Robert Grove: "I remember a grocery store where we always bought our groceries from out here in Boardman. It was Gifford's store. It was just a small building on the other side of the Y and S tracks, the southeast corner, just a small building."

Carl Ruckenbrod: "The only store in Boardman was the old Gifford and Laucks' grocery store. That was the location of the Boardman Supply Company and a man by the name of Merle Gifford became the Fire Chief. Gifford and Lauck's had a store that I don't believe was any bigger than a double garage and built pretty much the same as a double garage with a hip roof. They sold gas out front and it had a pretty good supply of groceries."

The Dispatch reported on November 21, 1923, that the Township Trustees received the new fire truck last week. It is mounted on a Ford truck, painted red, and with the ladders looks like the real thing. The fire station has been built back of Gifford-Loucks' store. The engine (chemical tank) has been charged and is all ready for use. Again, on January 16, 1924, the Dispatch reported, that the fire station building has been wired for electric lights and a siren put up to give the alarm when there was a fire. In addition to personal testimony as to the location of the first fire station, this hand-drawn map, obtained by John Darnell of the Boardman News in 1976, confirms that Gifford's gas and grocery store and the fire station building next to it were located as described in the LaLumia transcripts.

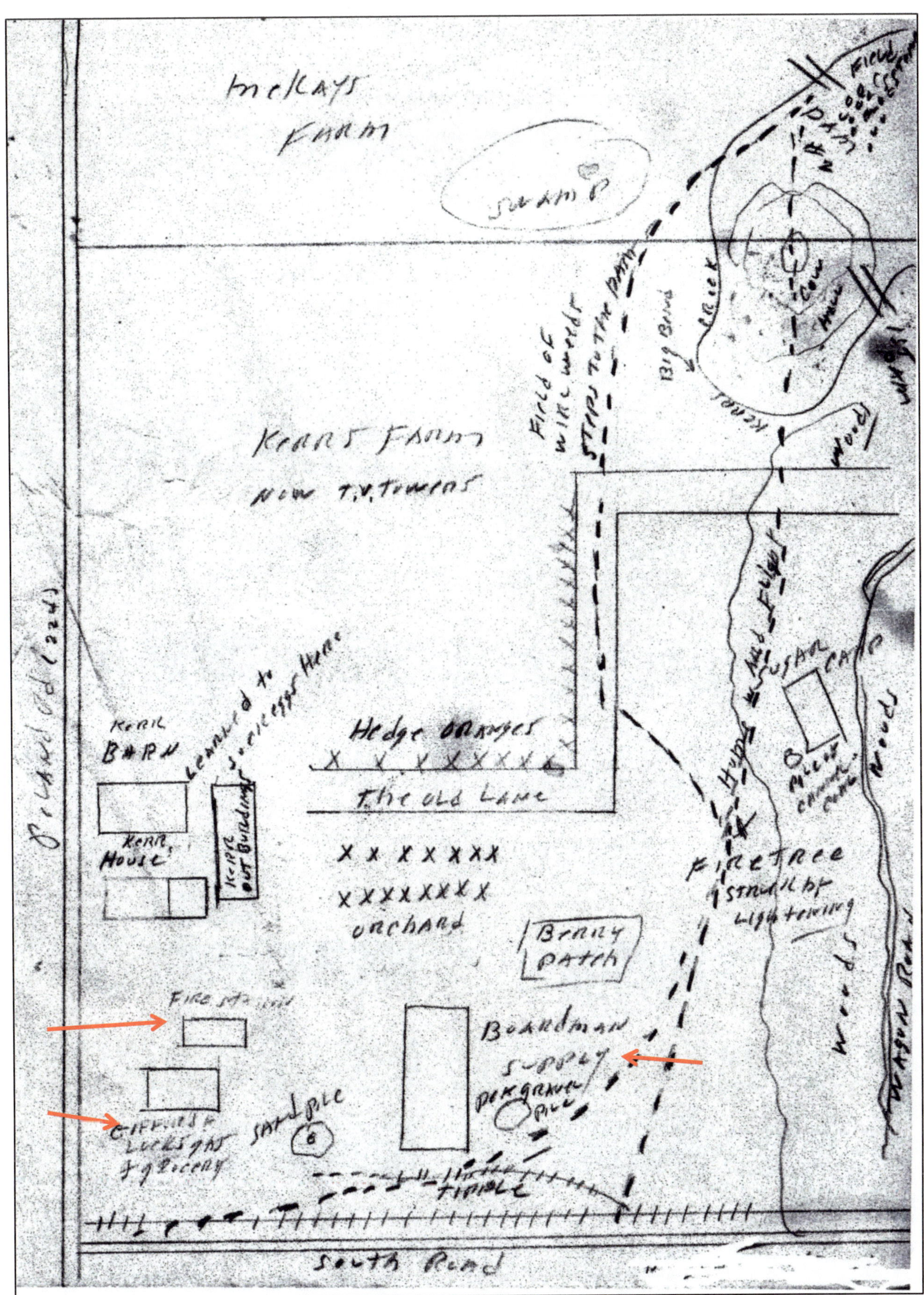
McKays
Farm
Swamp
Kerrs Farm
Now T.V. Towers
Field of wild weeds
Steps to the Dam
Big Bend
Creek
Cow
Dam
Woods
Hedge Oranges
The Old Lane
Kerr Barn
Kerr House
Kerr Out Buildings
Learned to suck eggs here
Orchard
Berry Patch
Fire Station
Boardman Supply
Sand Pile
Fire Tree
Struck by Lightening
Sugar Camp
Woods
Wagon Road
South Road
Tipple

Fire Station Number 1 located at 136 Boardman Poland Road- In 1927, the volunteers wrote a letter to the Trustees asking them to consider building a fire station to better serve the community in the future. The Trustees approved the project and accepted the bid from L. J. Clemmons to build the fire station for $7,250. The station was completed that year. The fire department had its first brick and mortar station. The station was located next to Chief Gifford's second grocery store. R.P. Smith, from Smith's Dairy, sold the property to the Township for $750.

Smith's Dairy Plant

Fire Station

Gifford's Grocery Store

Tommy Smith's Dairy Sales

Southern Boulevard

Rt. 224 east

Number 1 Station is to the left and the store in the background was the location of Chief Gifford's grocery store.

In 1936, the Trustees approved a one story addition to the fire station on the east side which added a second bay for a fire truck. In 1958, the Trustees approved the addition of a second floor to the station over the bay. This station was identified as Station Number 1 from 1927 to October 21, 1959, when the Trustees re-assigned it as the Number 2 Station making the station at 5105 Market Street the Number 1 Station where the Chief kept his office.

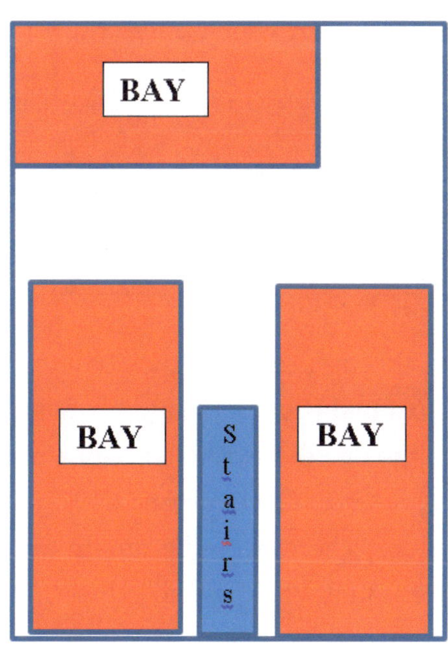

First Floor

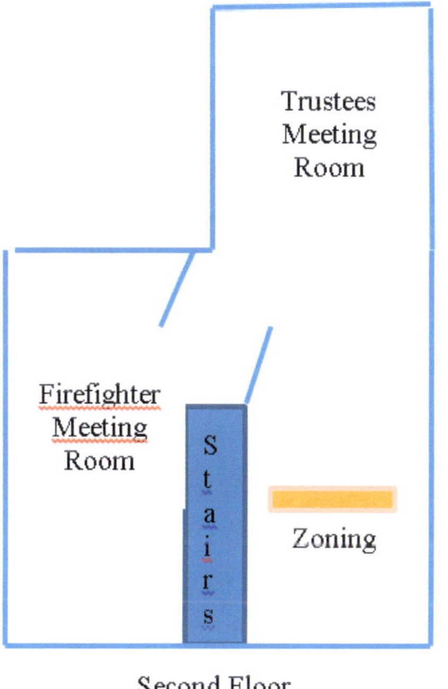

Second Floor

The International was in the rear bay and the GMC, the Civil Defense truck, was in the front left bay with the Mack in the front right bay. There was no kitchen and the bathroom was in the basement. During WWII, the firefighter meeting room was used to teach first aid to the citizens of Boardman.

In 1968, the Trustees approved the addition of four truck bays on the building's west side. This also provided an office for Chief Cover plus a home for the ladder truck. The official opening day of the addition was July 20, 1969. On July 19, 1969, the fire station at 5105 Market Street was turned over to the police and 136 Boardman Poland Road became the Number 1 Fire Station.

Inside Station Number 1 downstairs in 1977.

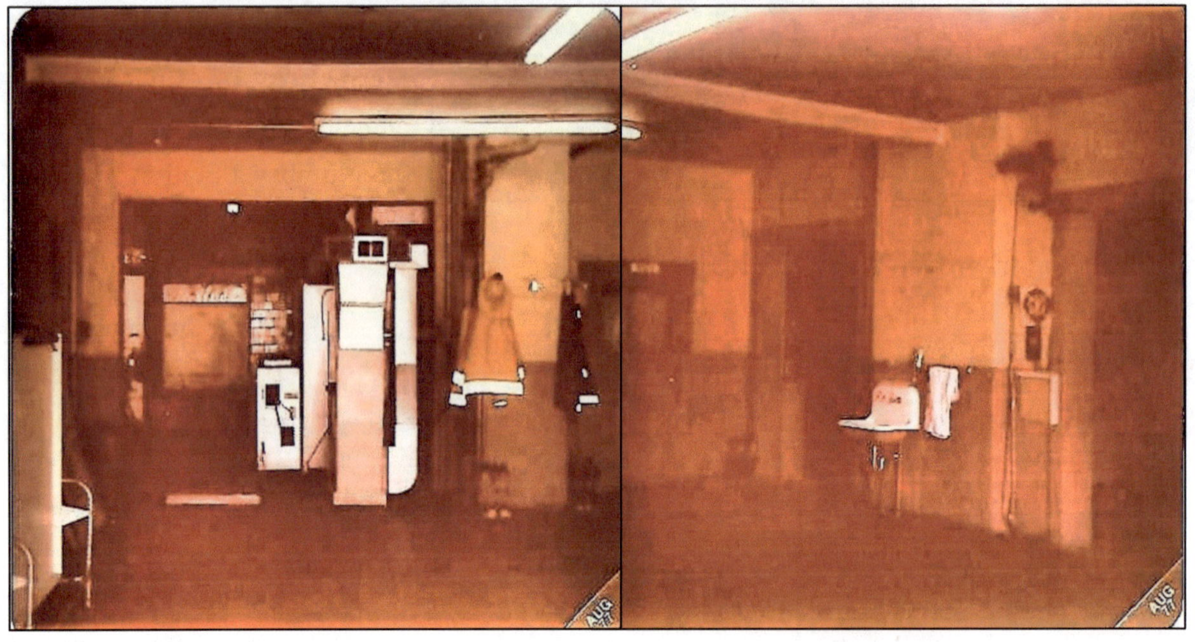

This view is what you would have seen if you entered the station through the first truck bay to the west. You would immediately see the heating unit straight ahead. Just to the left of the furnace system was the old hose washer that most firefighters would recognize as the one that was later relocated in the laundry area. Behind the hose washer was a small open bay where Chief Cover parked the Chief's car. The entrance was to the far left and was a single car garage door. There was a bathroom to the right rear. Just above the white porcelain sink is one of the klaxon horns that would sound in the station to let us know that a call was coming in. The floor was made of heavy oak planks that had dried out over the years to the point where you could see through the cracks down into the basement. Because the new fire trucks became heavier over the years, ceiling jacks had to be put into place to support the floor from sagging or collapsing. We were required to mop the floors daily with an old string wet mop.

If you happened to be in the basement when the floor was being mopped, you could get wet from the water dripping through the spaces between the floor planks.

On the left was the ping pong table. Many of the firefighters learned to play ping pong and we did it for hours in the evenings. Chief Cover was unbeatable. No one really wanted to play against him but he would entice us by telling us he would spot us 18 points, yet he would still beat us. His competition came from friends who were also top notch ping pong players. Friends such as John Garver and others would give the Chief a good game and provide us with entertainment as we watched the skilled players put on a show.

The two large openings to the right lead to the second bay which was the bay to the east. Its floor was of solid concrete as there was no basement under it. A weight bench and a set of weights were located at the rear of the bay. That was all that we had for physical fitness and workouts at that time. There were air banks to fill the SCBA bottles and oxygen bottles. There were four or five 4′ tall air bottles for the SCBAs and 3 slightly small green bottles to fill the O_2 bottles. An outside company would replace depleted bottles with full ones as needed.

The following picture is the same area of the fire station depicted in the two previous pictures: the bay with the heating system and the white porcelain sink are no longer there. This picture was taken forty years after remodeling.

The second floor of the station shows the aging and run-down living quarters. We look toward the front of the building with Route 224 just outside of the windows. In the back of the picture was the living room and in front was the dining area. The steps from the first floor came up on the left. The area, out of sight, to the far left, once served as the bunk room. Before that, it was the meeting room for the Trustee's bi-weekly meetings and the zoning inspector's office. In 1977, the bunk room was in the rear of the building. Before the station was remodeled, the windows had gotten so bad that when the wind blew, the curtains blew inward.

This was the bunkroom located at the rear of the building. There were six bunks. The Assistant Chief, Captain, and all other firefighters slept in this room. On the wall to the left was a desk where the Assistant Chief would answer the phone from the dispatcher so that we would know what type of call was coming in and where it was located. There was a blackboard on the wall near the phone. The Assistant Chief would write the address and circle the signal number to let us know the type of call; 55 for a house fire, 56 for a car fire, 57 for a grass fire, or signal 59 for a first aid call. A klaxon horn was located in the hallway just outside of the bunkroom. It would have been difficult for anyone to sleep through the horn going off at 2:00 in the morning.

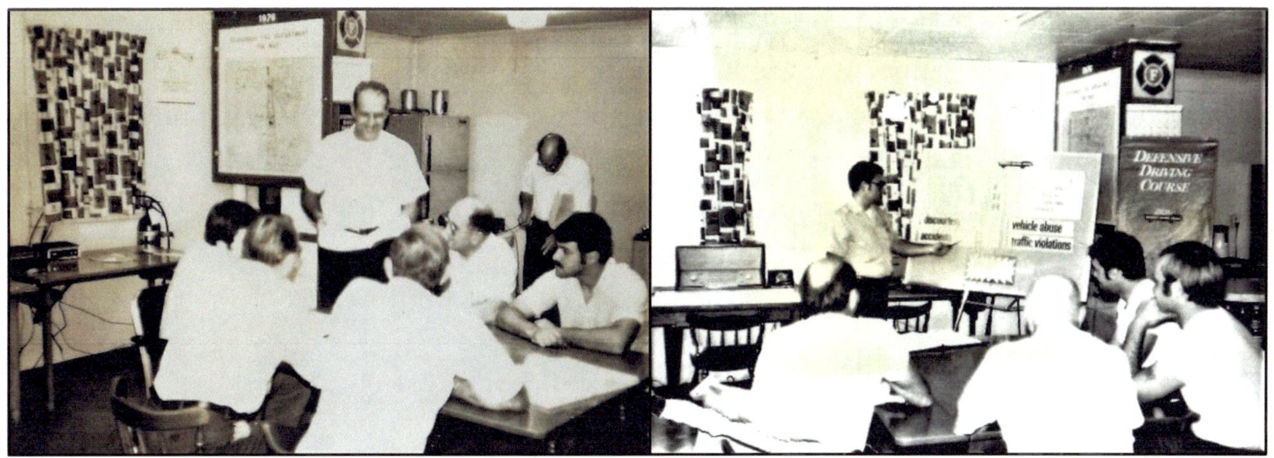

Kitchen and dining area. The two people standing are Assistant Chief Tomalka and Chief Cover.

Dan Lewis teaching Driver Training

Clockwise are Jim Dorman, Joe Ignazio, Bob Davis, Mark Moorhead and Assistant Chief Bill Bush.

Joe Ignazio preparing for Canfield Fair display in the downstairs east truck bay. In the background is the air fill station.

The bunkroom wall has the house phone, fire phone and siren pull box. There is a small wall desk to take notes when the calls come in.

In 1977, the Trustees approved a remodeling project which provided improvements to the living conditions inside the fire station. New windows as well as paneling were added to the building to give it a more modern look. The firefighters, with the permission of Chief Cover, carefully pealed the paneling from the walls of the former Trustees' meeting room and used them to cover the walls of the living room. Everyone was pleased with the results.

In 2004, this overhead shot was taken of Fire Station 71 at 136 Boardman-Poland Road.

This was once the location of Boardman's Clerk and Fiscal Office. The building was torn down, the lot paved, and used for parking.

The previous Road Department and Maintenance Garage.

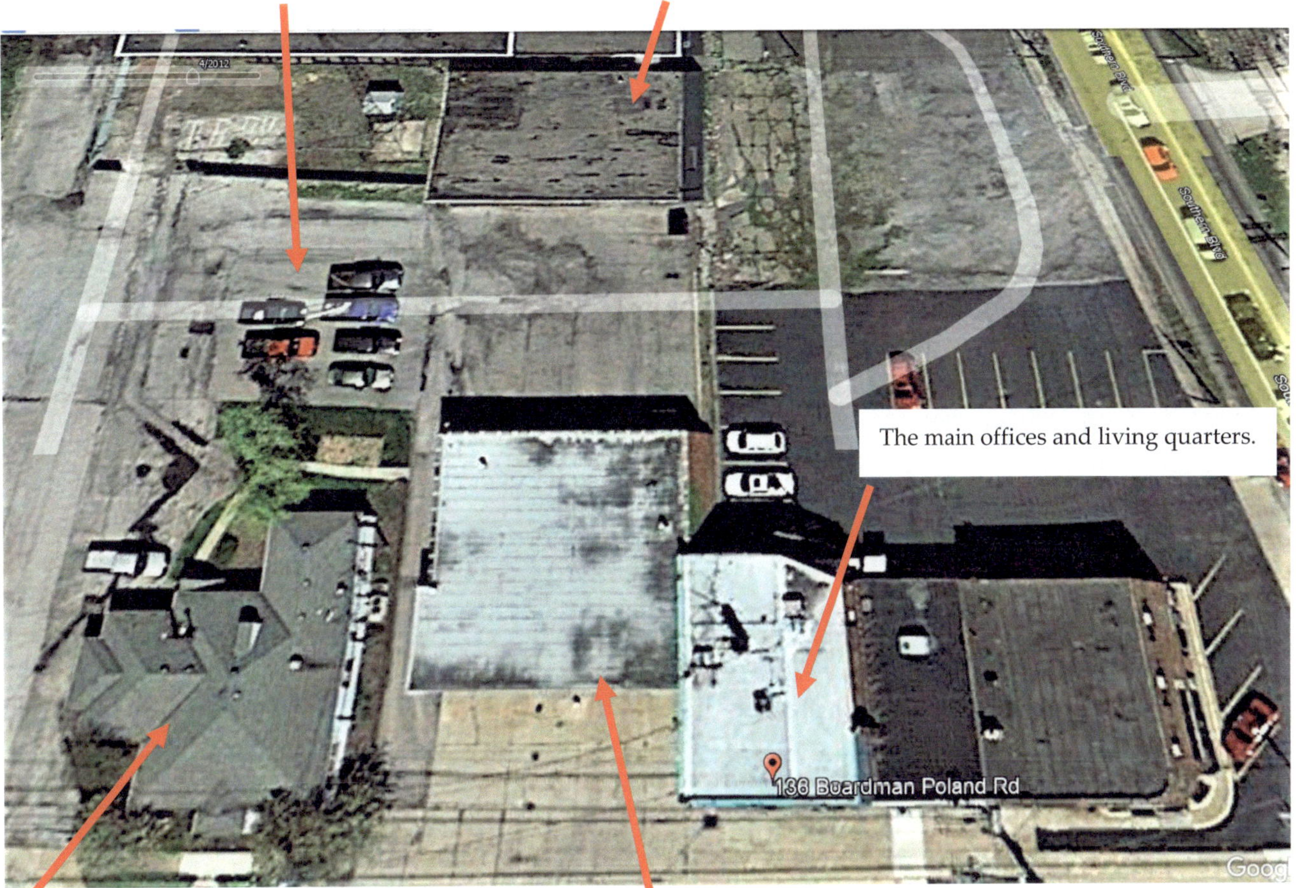

This building was formerly a restaurant, the Trustee's meeting hall, and in 2004, served as the Fire Prevention Office.

Four apparatus bays, double depth. Chief Cover had the roof poured with 4" of concrete anticipating a second floor would be added in the future. But when the day came that he requested the addition, Trustees turned him down.

The End of an Era

By 2018, after 93 years of service to the community, this fire station had served its purpose and was in serious need of upgrades to provide safe living quarters and to meet the needs of the community into the future. It was deemed less expensive to build the main station at another location rather than make costly upgrades to the old building.

The property was sold to help finance the new construction. Since Chief Mark Pitzer was not on the department at the time that the building was covered in paneling he had no way of knowing what lay beneath the exterior paneling. I met with him and pointed out that underneath were items that may be of historical value to our department. I told him that if they had not been damaged or lost in the remodeling, there was likely a three foot sandstone block inscribed with BFD and up to six sandstone keystones.

He was immediately energized by the possibility of retrieving these items of great historical value to our department. That same day, he directed the firefighters to examine the front of the building and they located the BFD stone and one keystone.

The firefighters marked the location of the two artifacts on the paneling to help find them in the future.

While the new fire station was in the design phase, Chief Pitzer was able to incorporate the sandstone block and the keystone into the new fire station's exterior design. Both items were successfully retrieved from the old building and nicely built into the front facing wall of the new fire station.

The Final Chapter of Fire Station Number 1 was written on April 2, 2020. The station was scheduled for demolition to make way for a gas station. After serving us so well for almost 100 years, the last walls of our fire station were torn down.

There is one shining light in the final days of our fire station. I was able to retrieve one last keystone from the front of the fire station before it all collapsed into a cloud of dust and debris. As the operator pulled back the siding with the gripper on the shovel, a keystone appeared.

The shovel operator was able to nudge the keystone loose and one of the demolition crew members retrieved the stone and delivered it to the rear of my SUV.

We were sad to see our historical building turned into another service station.

New Fire Station Number 71 located at 7440 Market Street- When it was decided to decommission 136 Boardman Poland Road, the search was on for a new location. The Trustees forged an agreement with the local school board. The school property, adjacent to Center Middle School at Market Street and Stadium Drive, was chosen for the new location. The property met the needs of the fire department in both size and location. The property was big enough to accommodate the new fire station and the location met the need to be within the zone that had the highest rate of emergency responses in the Township. A corridor running along Route 224 from West Boulevard east to Southern Boulevard has more calls than anywhere else in the Township. The high rate of calls within this corridor has not changed in the 25 years that these calls were recorded. The new main fire station would be built in a location to provide the quickest response to the area experiencing the most fire and EMS calls.

The BFD stone and keystone were placed in their new home by the stone masons.

A New Fire Station Under Construction

ANNOUNCING THE GRAND OPENING OF
BOARDMAN FIRE DEPARTMENT
STATION 71

Join us in celebration
Tuesday, May 29th from 6pm-8pm
7440 Market Street

Ribbon cutting at 6pm
Light refreshments will be served

ROBERT K. YOSAY | THE VINDICATOR

Current and former Boardman Township officials cut the ribbon Tuesday to open the new $3.6 million fire station at Market Street and Stadium Drive. Construction began last spring, and the project has been a decade in the making.

A Vindicator article dated Tuesday, May 29, 2018, reports, "Ninety-one years ago, the Township opened its first fire station. Now pieces of that station are memorialized in the fire department's new home on Market Street. The Township officially opened the new Station 71 on Tuesday with ribbon-cutting and an open house event. Although the construction of the $3.6 million facility at Market Street and Stadium Drive began last spring, Township officials said the project has been a decade in the making. Officials have long wanted to move the fire department out of the old building on U.S. Route 224. The chance to do so came, in part, due to a deal made between the Township and school district in which the two swapped properties saving money on the project. The location of the new station addresses response times to the southern end of the Township. The building's features include a training room, training tower, individual bunk rooms, and a storage room. Also in attendance were two retired Township Fire Chiefs, Jim Dorman, and George Brown. Dorman shared some of the department's history. He read from the 1926 Township Trustee's minutes that set in motion plans for the first fire station which was built in 1927. He also noted that features of the old building, including an original stone inscribed with "BFD," were incorporated into the new building. The new station preserved the department's past, while also moving it into the future."

Ready to serve

ROBERT K. YOSAY | THE VINDICATOR

Boardman fire chiefs past and present – Jim Dorman, left, Chief Mark Pitzer and George Brown – attended Tuesday's opening of the township's new $3.6 million station No. 71 on Market Street next to Stadium Drive.

The lobby has many interesting items both current and nostalgic.

The rubber fire coat and pants are nearly 100 years old. The rubber coat was donated by former Assistant Chief Barney Davison.

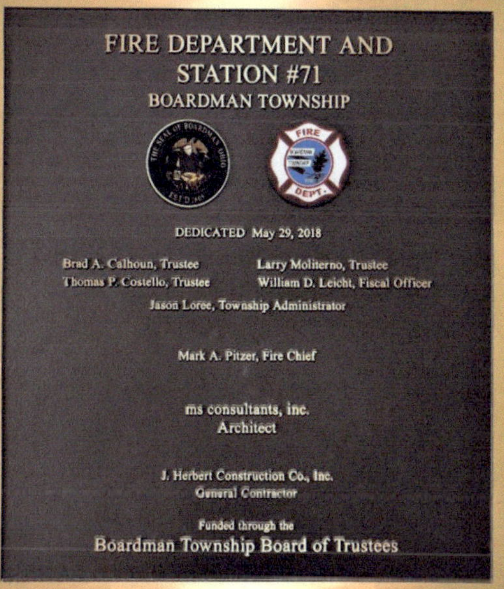

The bell, bulldog, and logo from the 1941 Mack truck.

Training room

Chief Pitzer's office

Workout room

Living room

Kitchen

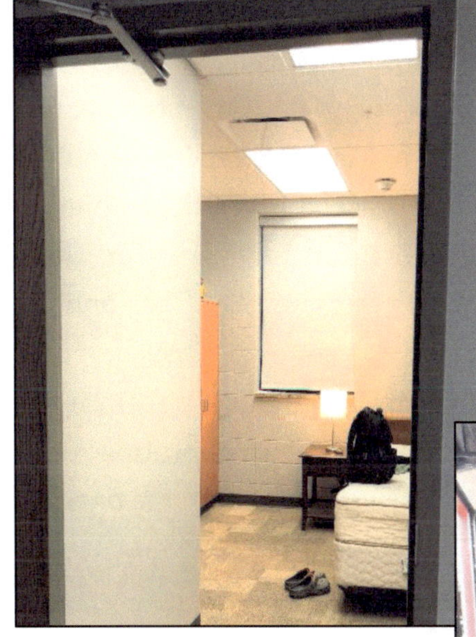

Individual bunkrooms

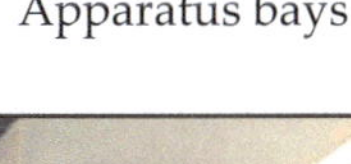

Apparatus bays

Mezzanine storage area

As he was working on a new fire station design, Fire Chief Mark Pitzer envisioned a memorial to fallen police officers and firefighters. He wanted the memorial to be built on the property of the new station located at Market Street and Stadium Drive. He asked two retired Chiefs to Co-Chair a fund-raising effort. Jerre Patterson former Police Chief and Jim Dorman former Fire Chief accepted the challenge to raise the funds. The memorial would be built entirely from donations. The committee first met in March 2018. A design was accepted and the Memorial Committee began soliciting funds from the public and local organizations. When the funding goal was met, work began on the project.

The memorial was dedicated on September 11, 2019. The Safety Service Memorial featured two wings; one each for the police and fire departments to honor their fallen members. Our department, fortunately, had lost only two firefighters in its 100-year history. On dedication day, we honored Bob Bonser and Phil Kibler. Bob Bonser died of a heart attack after being stricken at work on August 17, 1963. Phil Kibler was stricken by a heart attack after leaving Number 4 Station at the end of his shift, on December 10, 1982.

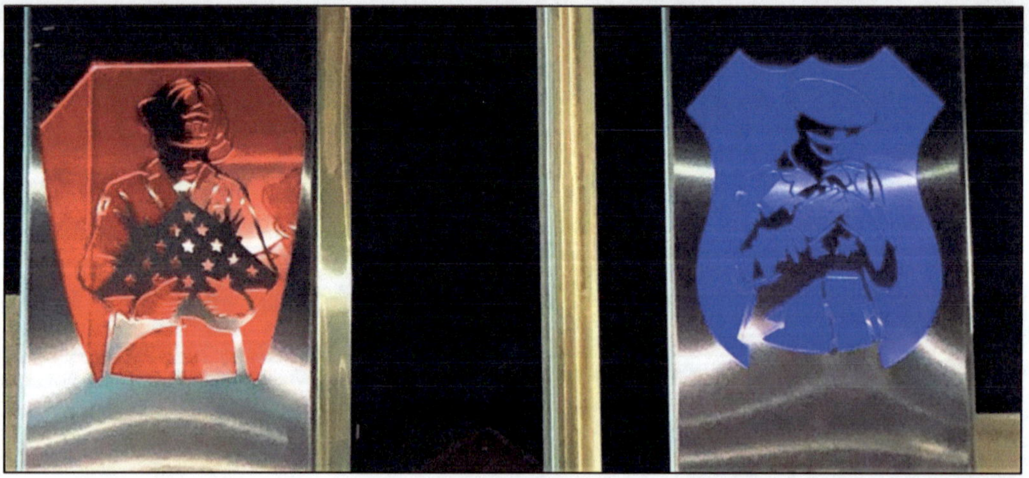

The following individuals, foundations, organizations and companies made significant contributions to the Fire & Police Memorial: Blasco Landscaping, Compco, Denise York, Edison Lighting, MS Consultants, OT Beight, Western Reserve Building and Trades Council, Aqua Ohio, Boardman Firefighters Local 1176, Boardman FOP, Boardman Kiwanis, Boardman Lions Club, Captured Moments Art, Fox Funeral Home, Boardman Poland Knights of Columbus, Boardman Poland Junior Woman's League, J. Ford Crandall Foundation, Lencyk Masonry, Margaret Mater, Operating Engineers Local 66, Petitti Garden Center, Phantom Fire Works (Bruce Zoldan), Walmart Foundation #2211, Joanne Wilhelm, Father Venglarik Council 11915, and Knights of Columbus.

Fire Station Number 2 later Number 1, 5105 Market Street

Barney Davison worked at **Fire Station Number 2** located at 5105 Market Street which was built in 1937 by the WPA. One of his duties was to man the dispatch desk. Because he also dispatched for the police department, Don Robinson, the Police Chief wanted to make the fireman dispatchers more official, so he produced an I.D. for each so that they could legitimately dispatch the police.

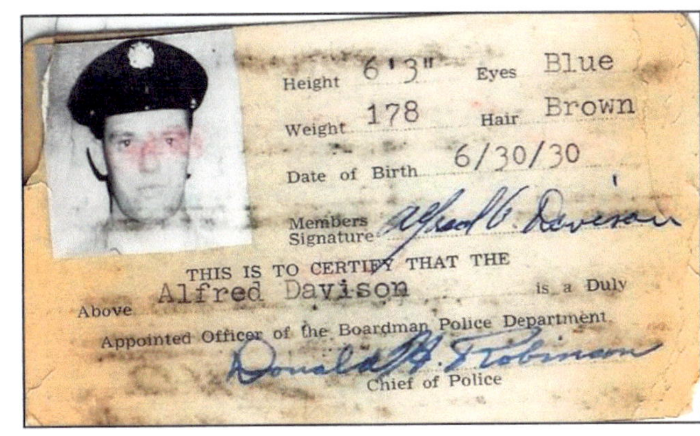
Height 6'3" Eyes Blue
Weight 178 Hair Brown
Date of Birth 6/30/30
Members Signature
THIS IS TO CERTIFY THAT THE
Above Alfred Davison is a Duly
Appointed Officer of the Boardman Police Department
Chief of Police

Look above the word "Fire" on the station sign for this Marquee.

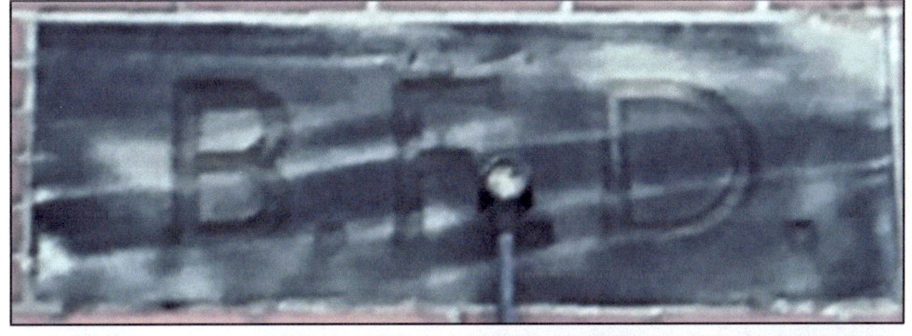

This stone is a duplicate of the stone set into the front wall of 136 Boardman Poland Road. It remains in the 5105 Market Street building.

The other stones were added to signify the building was a WPA project in 1937.

Our first two-way radio.

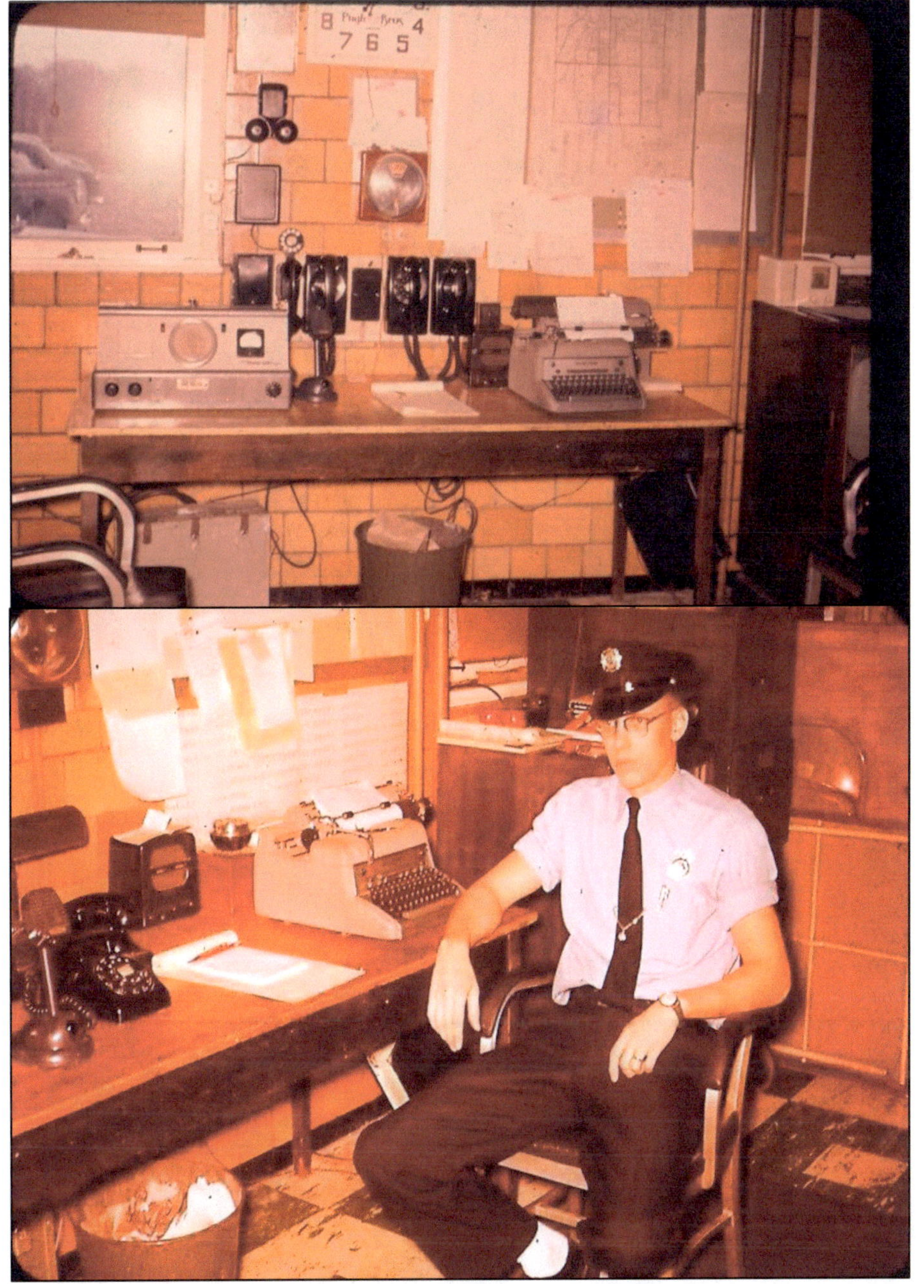

In 1957 the non-emergency phone number at Station Number 2 was SK8-2617.

Station Number 2 was opened in 1937. It was built for $32,000.

Starting in 1923, fire calls were sent directly to the Fire Chief's home and grocery store. The Chief or any clerk would answer the phone and get the necessary information from the caller. Then someone would go out to the siren on the telephone pole and push the button to "blow the whistle" to summon the firemen to the fire station to man the truck.

Davison described how a fire emergency was reported in 1955: the person discovering a fire would call the fire emergency phone number. Davison or another dispatcher would answer the phone and get the nature of the call, and location. He would then dial into what was called the code phone, which was similar to a party line phone. About 10 firemen could dial this private number at the same time. When the firefighters heard the fire siren, they would dial the code number. The dispatcher would announce the nature of the call and the address.

As the dispatcher was making the call he would pull the lever on the fire box and set off the siren. The dispatcher had two pull boxes: one each for Number 1 and Number 2 Station. Firefighters were assigned to specific stations. They only responded within their designated territory unless the fire was very bad. When this system was initiated, the territories were divided north and south of Ewing Road and Mathews Road The territories changed as the Township grew and fire stations were added.

The Alarm Box has three alerting positions. You would place the pin in the hole corresponding to how long you wanted the siren to blow. In the top position, a pull of the arm would get you a single rise and fall of the siren for a test (which occurred nightly at 6:00). The second position down would get you 2-3 rises and falls of the siren and the bottom position would get you 10-12 rises and falls of the siren which is what you would want if you were trying to get the attention of the volunteers to respond to a fire.

Chief Gifford moved into the upstairs of Station Number 2 not only for his office but also made his home there. After the Chief moved out of the fire station, he lived on Meadowbrook Avenue.

When Chief Gifford moved out, the station was configured like this for the first and second floors.

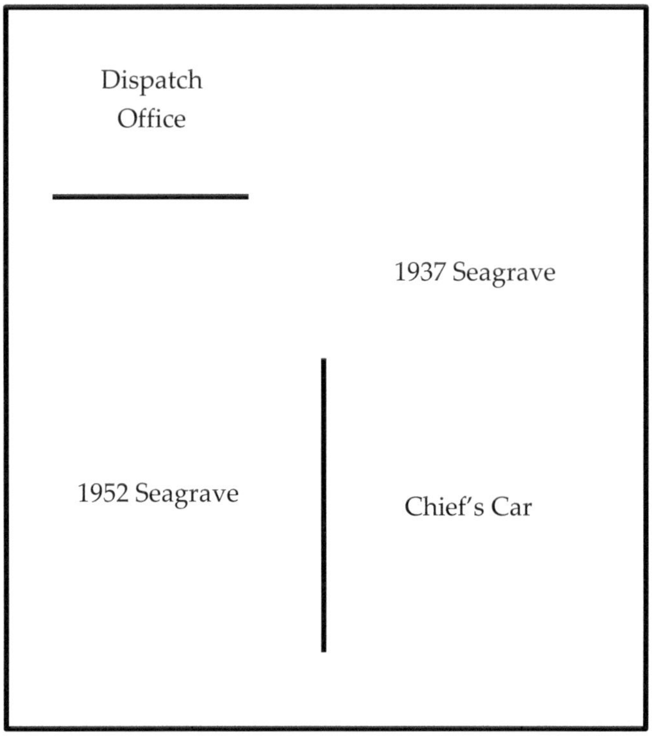

Dispatch
Office

Ground Floor

1937 Seagrave

1952 Seagrave

Chief's Car

Chief
Gifford's
Office

A/C Office

Big living room with
television

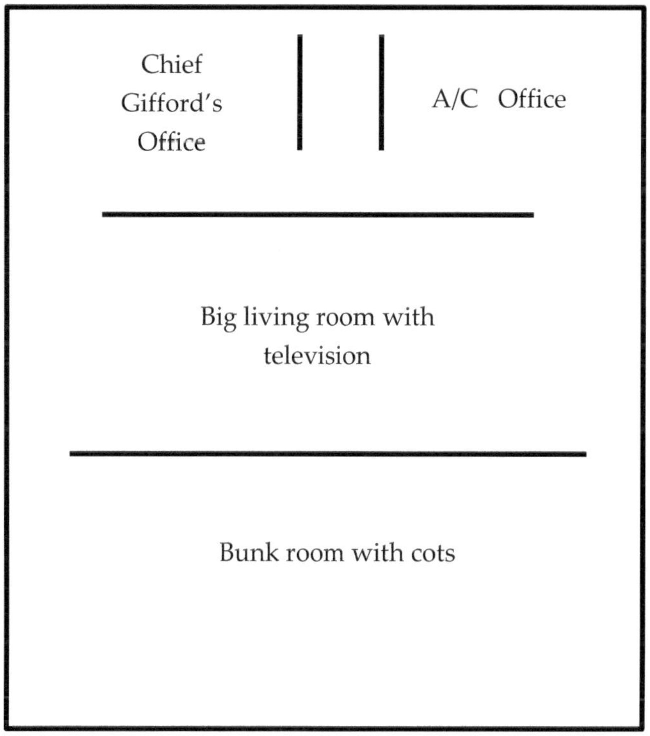

Second Floor

Bunk room with cots

Assistant Chief Bill Bush remembers a typical response to a fire call in the early fifties.

When a car fire or a grass fire was reported, one of the firefighters at Number 1 would get in the truck to respond while the other firefighter remained on the radio desk. The firefighter on the desk would tone out the radio sets and request all volunteer firefighters to respond. To tone out the volunteers, the dispatcher would send a high-pitched tone over the radio. The high-pitched tone would turn on the monitor radios of volunteers at home who would then be notified to respond to the fire. If a house fire came in and Lucy Gifford was home, both firefighters would respond (including the man on the radio) and she would take responsibility to become the dispatcher. She would then tone out the volunteers. For a house fire, one of the volunteers would respond to Number 2 Station and drive the firefighter on the desk to the fire if he hadn't already left.

Davison said that the radio call sign for the fire/police radio was KQC687. There was a base radio eventually placed at the Number 1 Station on Route 224 and one at Number 3 Station at Lockwood Boulevard and Shields Road. The call sign for that base radio was KQK-491. There was also a line called the LPL or Local Private Line. It looked like a regular phone. When the dispatcher picked up the LPL or anyone from any of the three fire stations picked up the LPL, it automatically set off horns in all three stations. This was used to quickly notify the other fire stations of an emergency. At Station Number 1, we had dual horns. The horns were in the hallway that ran from the living room to the bunk room. No one who was sleeping failed to hear these horns go off. The Number 2 Station non-emergency phone number at that time was ST8-9684.

Boardman eventually abandoned this location as a permanent fire station and turned the building over to the police department. The basement of the old fire station became the location of the first jail cells in the Township.

A second floor was added to the rear of the fire station. It was likely completed in 1959 when it was reassigned as Station Number 1 and the Chief began using the building as his headquarters.

Station Number Changes. This station was identified as Station Number 2 when it was built in 1937. On October 21, 1959, the Trustees re-assigned it as the Number 1 Station when Chief Gifford made this station the location of his office. They designated the station at 136 Boardman Poland Road Station Number 2. It had previously been Station Number 1.

On July 19, 1969, an addition of four bays was completed at the 136 Boardman Poland Road fire station. The addition included a new office for Chief Cover. With the relocation of the Chief's office to this site, it was re-named Station Number 1. July 20, 1969, was the last day of operation as a fire station for 5105 Market Street. On this date, it was turned over to the police department.

The fire station building was sold several times and used as a business office for the next fifty years. In 2019, the building was purchased by a gentleman who wished to remodel and convert the fire station into a bed and breakfast. He tried to keep as much of the building original as possible, presenting a fire station theme for the building. In 2021, he opened for business. The building was called the Red Door and featured bedrooms, a kitchenette, and a day room. One jail cell was available to lock up those who misbehave.

Historic 1937 Red Door Firehouse (New Listing!!!)

★ 4.50 (4 reviews) ·

Youngstown, Ohio, United States

Entire house
hosted by Philip

$371 / night
★ 4.50 (4 reviews)

Check availability

Construction of Fire Station Number 3 located at 1200 Shields Road was approved by Trustees early in the year. They awarded the contract for building the station to the Austin Construction Company. The firm's bid was $39,482. "The property was purchased over a year ago," according to an article in the Vindicator. The station was opened around September 15, 1959.

Open New Boardman Fire Station to Public Saturday

This is Boardman Township's new fire station at Shields Road and Lockwood Blvd. which will serve the township area west of Mill Creek Park. It has facilities for a captain and four firemen who will man it 24 hours. Located on an acre of ground, Fire Station No. 3 will be open for inspection by the public from noon to 9 p.m. Saturday. The building contains an apparatus section, dormitory, kitchen, alarm and general offices.

10-30-59

Before the construction of Number 3, Barney Davison, JB deSaulles, and Chief Gifford scouted out the empty property at the corner of Lockwood and Shields to try and figure out how to configure the fire station on the property. Chief Gifford was set on a two-bay apparatus bay that was double depth. He was planning for the day that the fire department would have its first aerial fire truck. Five full-time men were assigned to the station. The extra length would be needed for a long ladder truck. They worked with the architect Chet Long.

11/22/1959- The new fire station on Shields Road is now in full operation with four firemen stationed there: Bill Bush, Harley Carter, Charles Tomalka, and Captain Barney Davison. The 1952 Seagrave pumper was placed at Number 3.

11-1-59

Youngsters Look Over Boardman's New Fire Statio

Inspecting facilities at the new Boardman Township Fire Department open house Saturda afternoon were Gretchen Hoffman, 10, of 5026 Lockwood Blvd. and Arthur Carlson, 8, o 124 Willis Ave., pictured here with Assistant Chief Wayne Ewing. The new station, the depart ment's third, cost $45,000 and will serve the area west of Mill Creek Park. About 100 friend of the department were guests at a dinner Saturday night at Johnny Garneau's Restauran Among those present were fire officials from neighboring communities and also from Cleve land. Toastmaster John Moses introduced Chief Merle Gifford and members of his depart ment and other dignitaries.

The people who attended the open house for Station Number 3 signed this guest book.

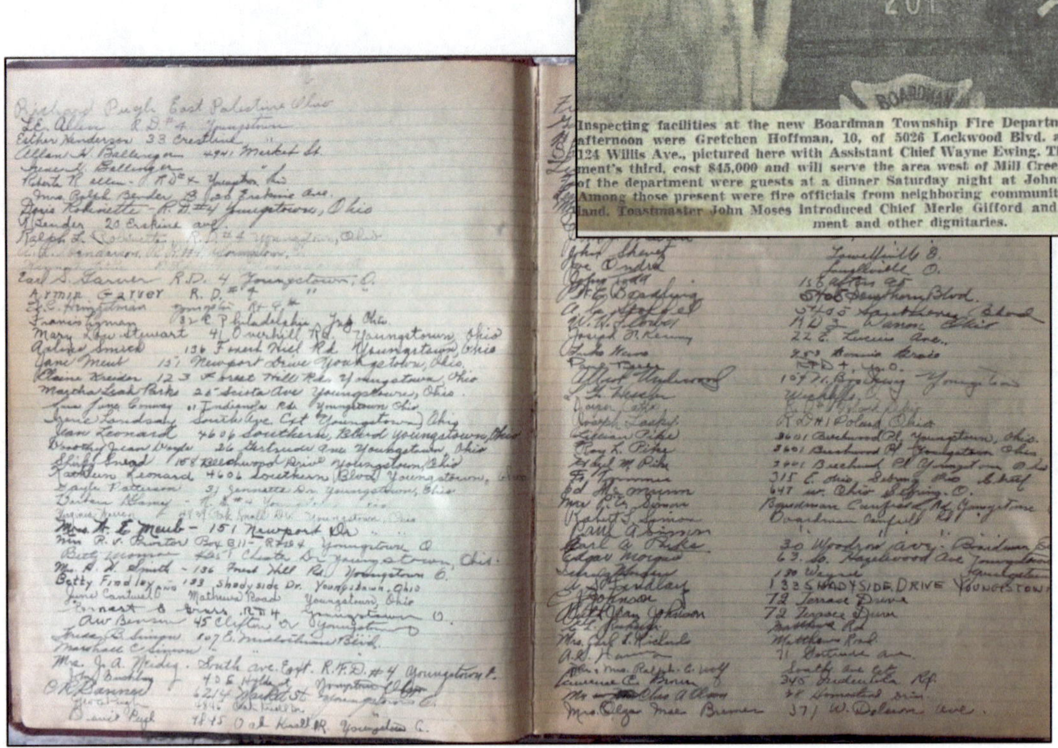

The station got its water for showers and the toilet from a cistern behind the station. After dumping their 500-gallon tank into the cistern, the crew from Number 3 would take their truck down to a nearby fire hydrant on Lockwood Boulevard for a refill. Drinking water was available from a drinking fountain supplied with bottled water.

Barney Davison and Harley Carter were working at Number 3 when the first fire this station should have been sent to occurred. The dispatcher notified the stations that there was a fire call on Shields Road near Tippecanoe Road. The officer-in-charge sent Number 2 Station to the fire. Harley looked out the front door in time to see a barn on fire on Shields Road. Both Davison and Carter stood out front as the Seagrave from Number 2 Station truck raced by. Afterward, Chief Gifford questioned Davison why he did not respond to the call. Barney said that he had been trained too well by Gifford. They were trained by Gifford not to do anything unless ordered to do so. "That was the end of that," said Davison.

The doors to Station 3 were much bigger than the ones at Station 1 and were two bays deep. When an aerial ladder truck was purchased in 1966, it was clear that the trucks had outgrown the main fire station. The ladder was assigned to Station 3 because it would fit through the doors. When the ladder was needed, the Station 3 crew would take it instead of the pumper truck. The truck was not located where it was most needed, but it was parked in the only building where it would fit. In 1969, Chief Cover had four bays added to the main station providing a proper location for the aerial ladder.

In 2002, Township Trustees took stock of the aging fire stations. Station Number 1 was 75 years old and it was over 25 years since it had last been remodeled. This station had serious infrastructure problems with mold being one of the worst issues. It lagged behind any modern version of health, safety, and functionality. Stations Number 3 and 4 were over 40 years old and outside of a small amount of space added at Station 4, both stations were lacking in functionality and needed modernizing. Station Number 4 was too small for two firefighters and was not able to accommodate a growing fire department. After consideration, the Trustees chose to remodel Station 3 and build a new Station Number 4.

Remodeling Began In August of 2003, the ground was broken on the projects for both Stations 73 and 74. Station 73 would have square footage added and existing living spaces were remodeled. Station 74 would be razed and a new station built in its place. Here is a look at the progress of the renovation and the addition made to Station Number 73.

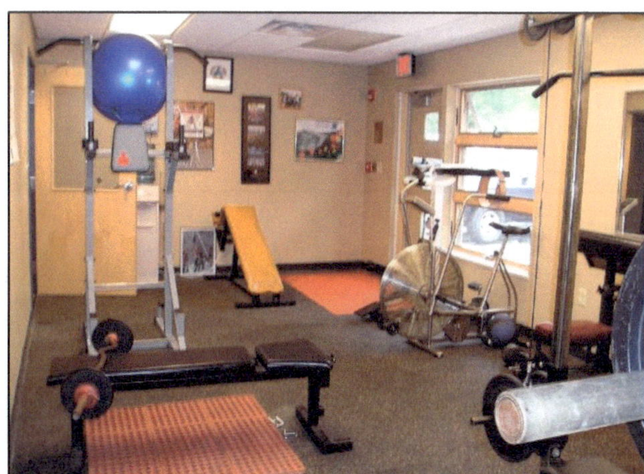

Station 73 was remodeled for $450,000 and has 6,236 square feet. The station was built with six bed rooms. The station, at the time of the opening, had 3 firefighters assigned. The additional bedrooms were built because it was reasoned that it was less expensive to make room for additional firefighters now rather than years later.

Fire Station Number 4

Temporary Fire Station Number 4 located on Boardman Poland Road just east of South Avenue- Barney Davison said that Ohio Insurance Service Office which regulates insurance rates, required that Boardman secure a location for a fire station to serve the eastern portion of the Township to keep residents, in that area, within 3 miles of a fire station. Subsequently, the Township Trustees, on January 30, 1961, passed a motion to temporarily rent space to house a fire truck. Also, an undated newspaper article states, "Temporary fire station to bring the Township within the 3 mile limit governing fire insurance rates." A temporary fire station opened at Route 224 just east of McKay's Corners. (South Avenue and Boardman Poland Road)

- The Township rented a single vehicle garage from Paul Good. It was barely big enough to hold the International pumper that was parked in it.
- Paul Good was given a Plectron radio monitor so that when the tones went off, he could leave his father's garage, located on Route 224 just east of South Avenue, and head to the rented garage and take the International to the call.
- The rent paid on the garage was $1,200 per year the same as they had been paying Poland for service.

The article continues;" Good's Garage was rented to house a fire truck. The volunteer firemen will man a truck from that location. Poland had previously signed a contract for $1200 to provide this coverage. Another newspaper article states, "Last week Boardman Township Trustees discontinued arrangements with Poland Volunteer Fire Department for Poland to service homes on the edge of Poland but are in Boardman Township." The article points out "a truck has been placed at Good's Service but this station will not be open or manned at night and will have no trained firemen available at any time. Trustees are to purchase land in the Mathews Road area later for a permanent station. Considering long range growth, Trustees purchased land at South Avenue. and Walker Mill Road for an additional station." The Trustees never sold the Walker Mill and later placed an emergency siren on the property.

The Trustees anticipated the need for a station to cover the eastern regions of the Township. In preparation for this station, Trustees slowly purchased property in the area as it became available. In the early stages of making plans, the Trustees were very unsure of the best location for this station. In February of 1958, they bought property at Indianola Road and Simon Road. This was followed by purchases in March and April of properties located at South Avenue and Mathews Road and South Avenue and Walker Mill Road. According to former Assistant Chief Barney Davison, "There was a big debate over this since it was determined by studies that the traffic and traffic flows were difficult at South Avenue and Mathews Road. The proximity to Robinwood School could pose a danger to school children who walk to school. The neighbors in the vicinity of South Avenue and Walker Mill Road said they did not want a fire station in the neighborhood. With all of this in mind, 6169 South Avenue was chosen as the location for Station 4.

Fire Station Number 4, located at 6169 South Avenue was built in 1961 for $15,000.

This station was built to provide fire protection to the east side of Boardman Township. A newspaper article dated March 28, 1961, states, A bulldozer begins clearing brush at a site on South Avenue one quarter mile south of Mathews Road The station will hose one truck and one man. The station was slated to cost $15,000 and take two months to build.

Chief Wayne Ewing worked with the Kreider Construction Company to build the single bay fire station. Station Number 4 was built to provide fire protection to the Hubbard Estates neighborhood, just east of the freeway off Mathews Road. All areas of the Township were now covered.

Trustee Chairman H. W. Mansell said, "The station will house a single truck with sleeping quarters for one man at first. Later, the station will be enlarged. The station should be completed in about two months. A temporary station on Route 224 (Good's garage) will be discontinued." Good's garage was no longer used effective September 15, 1961.

Many firefighters often said that working in Station 4 was like working in an area the size of a postage stamp. It was small and took getting used to it. Trying to improve the tight living space, Chief Wilson had the front porch enclosed. With limited funds, he did the best he could to add to the living space, but firefighters still needed more space.

The bay doors at the fire station were fine for the size of trucks that were built in the sixties. They could easily drive through the front and rear doors and not be concerned that their mirrors may hit the door jambs. But that changed in the seventies as the newer fire trucks were all built wider and taller. The back door of Number 4 was narrower than the front. They could drive out of the front door easily but when returning from a call they drove in through the rear door. With the newer trucks, they had to move the side mirrors to get in the back door. Years later as even newer trucks were bought, the trucks were so wide, they were forced to back into the front door. The rear door was no longer an option.

In 2002, the decision was made to demolish Station Number 4 and build a much bigger station for the firefighters. To preserve a piece of the heritage the old fire station represented, two 18" X 18" sandstone blocks were removed so that they could be re-located on the new Station 4. Firefighters worked hard to remove two unblemished blocks from the old station. The work on the new fire station began in 2003.

Firefighters are removing a sandstone slab to be reset in the new fire station.

The progress of the new building.

A sandstone slab from the old station was re-installed in this pillar on the new station.

An aerial view of the project shows the old station before demolition in front of the new fire station.

October 14, 2004

4 Boardman Town Crier

Firefighters celebrate opening of stations

By Raymond L. Smith
Town Crier

BOARDMAN — With a new fire station #74 and a renovated fire station #73, Boardman Fire Chief James Dorman smiled as he said the department is looking ahead at convincing township council that its downtown fire station on State Route 224 also needs to be brought up to date.

"We would like the main station to get the same kind of overhaul as has been done at this location," Dorman said.

Boardman Trustee Tom Costello said the township is not looking at renovating the main station at this time, but could consider it in the future.

"What was done at these stations were big capital investments," he said.

On Thursday, Dorman focused his energies on the grand openings of the two stations and the unveiling of a new $43,000 fire safety mobile classroom that will be used to teach children and other community residents about fire safety. The fire department also is scheduled to receive a new pumper truck with a ladder.

Fire Station #73, 1200 Shields Road, now is 6,236 square-foot building, with six private bedrooms for the firefighters. The renovation cost the township $450,000.

Currently, there are three firefighters at the station on every shift.

Fire station #74, 6169 South Ave., is a brand new 7,643 square-foot building that cost the township approximately $900,000.

"We wanted to have enough space available in case the township decides that continued growth dictates that we need to add new firefighters at the stations," Dorman said.

Costello said the township decided to build the stations with six sleeping quarters now, because it is less expensive at today's costs than waiting years down the road when material and labor costs likely will go up.

Town Crier / Gabriel Crish

A fire truck sits outside of the new South Avenue Fire Station.

■ See Stations Page 10

BOARDMAN TOWNSHIP FIRE DEPARTMENT STATION 74

DEDICATED OCTOBER 2004

TOWNSHIP OFFICIALS

ELAINE R. MANCINI	CHAIR
THOMAS P. COSTELLO	VICE-CHAIR
KATHY MILLER	TRUSTEE
WILLIAM D. LEICHT	CLERK
CURT B. SEDITZ	ADMINISTRATOR
JAMES R. DORMAN	FIRE CHIEF
STROLLO ARCHITECTS, INC.	ARCHITECT

Station 74 was built for $940,000 and has 7,643 square feet. This station has two truck bays and was two bays deep. The extra space was added to accommodate additional fire trucks in the future and

provided indoor space to conduct training sessions. The station was built with six bedrooms.

In addition to the firefighters assigned to the station, there was a pumper truck and a 75′ quint. When a children's fire safety trailer was purchased, it was also parked at this station.

Fire Chiefs

Boardman Fire Department was organized in September of 1923 when a small group of civic minded men decided there should be a way to meet the growing need for a community fire department. These men, led by Merle W. Gifford, started Boardman's fire department and so began the legacy of Fire Chief Merle Gifford and those Fire Chiefs who followed.

Merle W. Gifford served the department from 1923 until 1961 as the first Fire Chief. Before he came to Boardman, Merle Gifford spent two years with Hubbard Fire Department. After Boardman, he spent five years as Chief of the Austintown Fire Department.

Under Chief Gifford's leadership, the township purchased its first fire truck, a 1923 Model T Ford. He became the first full-time paid firefighter. In 1927, he oversaw the construction of the first brick and mortar fire station on Boardman Poland Road near Southern Boulevard. Chief Gifford had Boardman's next fire station constructed in 1937, another in 1959, and the last one built in 1961. He was responsible for the purchase and installation of the first two-way radios. His worst fire on record was the Hitchcock barn burning to the ground in 1930. It was one of the largest barns in Ohio at the time. Gifford was 25 years old when he began working for the Township, making him the youngest Fire Chief Boardman has ever seen and his tenure of 39 years set a record that hasn't been broken.

The township's second Fire Chief, (Harold) Wayne Ewing, was appointed Chief in 1961 and served until 1965. He joined the fire department in 1954. Chief Ewing was said to have maintained the department responsibly and continued its growth. Chief Ewing upgraded the department's rescue abilities with the purchase of a rescue vehicle. During Chief Ewing's career, he experienced major fires in the township: a $250,000 fire at Aerolite Extrusions and the Boardman Lumber Yard fire in 1965 which caused $75,000 in damages.

Donald C. Cover joined the fire department in 1940 as a volunteer firefighter. In 1965, the Township Trustees appointed him its third Fire Chief at a salary of $575 per month. Cover quickly became a sought-out expert in arson investigations nationwide. He photographed many fire scenes, inside and outside of Boardman, cataloging more than 60,000 slides. Cover also improved the fire department in first aid and vehicle rescue. Chief Cover purchased the first ladder truck in 1965 for just under $64,000. He purchased the department's first set of vehicle rescue tools which included air chisels, a rescue saw, and the "Jaws of Life,"

Chief Cover was responsible for remodeling the main fire station, adding floor space to accommodate six fire vehicles. Also under his administration, Cover appointed the first Fire Prevention Officer. In 1974, the department fought a fire that destroyed the Arena Bowling Lanes on Simon Road and caused over $500,000 in damages.

4-28-41

I place my appliation to become a member of the Boardman fire dept with John Heintzleman

Don Cover
RFD#4
Yo. O.

John Brian "JB" deSaulles was the only man to serve as Fire Chief on two separate occasions. Also, when he was a junior firefighter, he was elected to the position of Chief for two years. In 1955, at the age of 18, he became a full-time firefighter. He was appointed as the Interim Fire Chief in 1965, for three months between Chief Ewing and Chief Cover and again for 14 months from 1985 until 1987 between Chief Cover and Chief Wilson. Although deSaulles' tenure was brief, he was credited with promoting the adoption of nationally recognized Fire Codes to enable the Fire Inspection Bureau to have the proper authority to ensure fire safety in township businesses and buildings. He was also responsible for hiring the department's first secretary to help with the growing amount of clerical work. deSaulles didn't escape large loss fires during his term as Chief; he was in command of the Rossi Furniture Store fire in the strip plaza at South Avenue and Mathews Road and a serious fire at the Bev Road Rehabilitation Workshop.

James E. Wilson became the township's next appointee to lead the fire department. He was appointed in January 1987 and served until 1996. He joined the full-time department in 1973. Chief Wilson's focus was to upgrade the fire department's tools and equipment by purchasing large diameter hose for improved water supply, purchased pagers used to call back firefighters when needed for additional manpower, and modernizing the alerting system for notifying stations of emergency calls. He was the first to introduce computers to the fire department. He introduced the first SOP document to the department. He purchased the department's first vehicle exhaust system as well as the first personal alerting safety system (PASS), a device worn by firefighters entering a burning building. An alarm would sound if a firefighter stopped moving for too long if incapacitated. In 1995, Chief Wilson purchased a 95' aerial ladder truck for $435,000 to replace an outdated aerial truck. One of Chief Wilson's noteworthy fires happened in 1987 when a fire with an estimated $2.5 million loss occurred at Stambaugh's Home Improvement Center in the Boardman Plaza. It was determined lightning struck the building, allowing the fire to get a head start and create a large volume of fire which required several mutual aid fire departments to respond and assist in extinguishing the fire. This fire still reigns as the largest dollar loss fire in the department's history.

In September 1996, James R. Dorman followed Chief Wilson as the sixth Fire Chief. Chief Dorman was a 24 year veteran of the department. He joined as a volunteer firefighter in 1968 and became a full-time firefighter in 1972. He served for six years as Captain and eight years as an Assistant Chief and retired in 2011. Chief Dorman's accomplishments include the upgrading of air packs and the air filling station, the replacement of a fire truck, the purchase of the department's first Thermal Imaging cameras, and the placing of the first AEDs on each apparatus. Chief Dorman formed a formal fire investigation team and purchased a vehicle and equipment to support the team. During his tenure, two fire stations received badly needed upgrades. The upgrades included the construction of a new Station 74 on South Avenue and the remodeling of Station 73 on Shields Road in 2004. Chief Dorman purchased enough portable radios so that each firefighter could have his own personal portable radio. Chief Dorman succeeded in adding two additional Fire Prevention Officers to total three in the office. In 2008, Township Trustees laid off nine full-time firefighters, nine volunteer firefighters, and one secretary due to budgetary shortfalls; the only time this has occurred in the department's history. Chief Dorman experienced his share of noteworthy fires, the $2-million Carpet Remnant Room arson fire in January of 1997 and the fire in Saint James Church at Boardman Park when lightning struck the steeple.

Tim Drummond served as the Interim Fire Chief upon Dorman's retirement. Drummond was the Fire Chief from April 1, 2011 to June 8, 2011, 68 days. He joined the department on May 20, 1985. In his short term in office, he kept fire operations running smoothly until George Brown took over. He experienced one serious fire as the commander, on April 26th. A major house fire occurred in the bedroom of a Prestwick Drive home which caused $165,000 in damages. Drummond was promoted to Captain in July of 1991 and Assistant Chief in September 1995.

Chief George Brown was appointed Chief on June 8, 2011, after serving with the Howland Fire Department as their Fire Chief for 12 years. Chief Brown was the only person in the 90-year history of the township appointed to the position of Fire Chief who came from outside the township. Among the initiatives Brown will be remembered for during his time as Chief is the purchase in 2012 of a 100-foot ladder truck, upgrading the radio system to an 800 MHz system with the cooperation of Humility of Mary Health Partners during the expansion of St. Elizabeth Hospital, and hiring 10 firefighters. Chief Brown implemented what he called the "No Child

Sleeps Unprotected" program. He secured funding from businesses and civic organizations for 750 smoke detectors. These were given to school children whose families couldn't afford to purchase smoke detectors for their homes. Chief Brown made great improvements in firefighter and officer training. The fire that stands out during Chief Brown's tenure was the $1-million fatal fire at the Lockwood Village Apartments in January 2013. Chief Brown was able to replace an aging aerial truck with a new 102' ladder truck from E-One.

In July 2014, the township selected Mark A. Pitzer to be its eighth Fire Chief. Chief Pitzer was hired as a firefighter in 2003 and became one of the 9 firefighters Chief Dorman was forced to lay off due to budget shortfalls. His appointment was noteworthy because he was the only person to be selected as Chief of the department without first having served as a fire officer in the department. His selection was, for the most part, due to his firefighting experience with the Fairfax VA Fire Department, his education and his vision for the future of the fire department. During Chief Pitzer's tenure, he adopted a new Fire Prevention Code, purchased two pumper trucks, one ladder truck, one command vehicle, and secured a vehicle for use as a brush fire vehicle. He updated the department's procedures and guidelines and oversaw the construction of a new modern fire station. He successfully promoted the idea of a memorial to fallen firefighters and police officers and directed the fundraising and construction of the commemorative structure. As with his predecessors, Chief Pitzer has not been immune to notable fires. There were two fatal fires: one in December 2015 on Border Avenue and another on Glenwood Avenue in April 2016. In 2020, he was forced to manage the fire department while dealing with a reduction in manpower due to the Covid-19 pandemic.

All Chiefs of Boardman Fire Department have left their mark on the department aiming to make a dangerous job as safe as possible for its firefighters while providing the citizens of Boardman Township with a quality, well trained, and progressive public service.

✠ Fire Prevention Bureau ✠

The job of a Fire Prevention Officer is not as glamorous as that of a firefighter but their job is very important. If you ask a Fire Prevention Officer why Boardman seems to have fewer fires than in the older days, they will quickly tell you the Fire Prevention Office can take a lot of the credit for this trend. To be sure, this claim is immeasurable but, no one could disregard the awesome things they have done for the community and the firefighters. They teach children how to be safe around fire. They inspect businesses, schools, and industrial buildings to make sure the fire codes are strictly followed. They make sure new building construction complies with current fire safety standards. They keep the officers and the firefighters up to date on potential hazards in the buildings in Boardman. They make sure that the big fireworks displays are shot off in a safe manner. They make sure the enormous underground fuel tanks are installed and buried in a manner to minimize the possibility of fuel leaks. They make sure that children in schools and senior citizens in nursing care homes live in the safest environment possible. In between, they respond to fire calls in the Township. Who wouldn't agree that they have contributed to a lower occurrence of fires? I believe they have helped all of Boardman to be a safer place to live and I thank them for what they do and believe they are vital to the well-being of the people and our buildings.

The first Fire Inspector was Captain Charlie Tomalka who convinced Chief Cover to use a spare vehicle so he could inspect schools to be sure they complied with the fire codes. He also spent time educating the grade school kids about fire safety. He conducted regular fire drills in the schools. Charlie Tomalka and his brother Jack (a Boardman volunteer firefighter) implemented giving grade school kids a ride in the bed of the 1941 Mack. Charlie Tomalka was never officially a Fire Inspector but he did the job because he felt strongly about keeping kids safe through fire education and enforcement of the fire codes. There were times when Charlie took the firefighters from his shift and had them tour the schools' layouts. Captain Tomalka was conducting inspections and providing kids with an education while on his normal firefighter shifts.

In 1974, the position of fire inspector became permanent and the newly appointed Fire Prevention Officer (FPO) Dan Lewis was assigned to work a 40-hour work week from 8:00 am until 4:00 pm. It was a lateral move from fire suppression. The pay was the same as a firefighter. The Fire Prevention Officers were called Fire Inspectors and Fire Prevention Officers in their earliest days. They were required to take a Civil Service test for the position. The benefit of taking the job was the schedule. Working 8 to 4 with nights and weekends off. The drawback was they were not permitted to work holidays (no businesses were open), so they were not eligible to receive holiday pay. Eventually, through contract negotiations, the FPO was given the rank of Lieutenant and their pay was elevated to halfway between that of a firefighter and a Captain. But, there were times an FPO had to follow up on inspections on a day off or work a duty such as evening fireworks shoots on the 4th of July. This provided them the opportunity to collect overtime pay for the extra work. Although not planned as a substitute, the overtime pay helped make up for the loss of holiday pay. Fire Prevention Officers over the years include:

Dan Lewis, Bob Davis, Francis Buckley, Jjm McCreary

Ken Pahon, Tom Roberts, Bill Glaser, Will Ferrando

James Yocum, Joel Wharry, Jeff Gallimore, Tom Donadee

There were many accomplishments made by Fire Prevention Officers but perhaps the most significant achievement was made by the first Fire Prevention Officer, Dan Lewis. Tomalka started with school inspections and teaching fire safety. But, it was Lewis who had to look at the whole Township with 43,000 residents and the center of shopping in the County and figure out how he was going to inspect buildings, enforce codes and provide fire safety training to the busiest community in the County, by himself. He requested Trustees to adopt the Ohio Fire Code so that he would have the authority to enforce codes. He had to review plans for new building construction. He had to set a schedule to inspect schools, motels, dry cleaners, businesses, and industrial buildings. He had to make time to inspect the installation of underground fuel tanks. He established all procedures to perform the duties his new job demanded. He determined the course of action for many Fire Prevention Officers to come.

Major accomplishments of the Fire Prevention Office:

- Boardman Township changed its fire codes from Ohio Fire Codes to the codes used by contractors for new construction, BOCA (Building Officials and Codes Administrators). While Francis Buckley was a Fire Prevention Officer, he and acting Chief JB deSaulles upgraded from the Ohio Fire Codes to provide the fire prevention office with better tools to enforce the codes. The BOCA fire codes were approved by the Township Trustees.
- They worked hand in hand with the general contractors who built the first and second seven-story towers at Saint Elizabeth Hospital Boardman Campus to assure compliance with fire codes.
- In conjunction with monitoring compliance with fire codes during Saint Elizabeth building construction, Fire Prevention Officers successfully negotiated with Saint Elizabeth Hospital (Mercy Health) the purchase of a new radio system for Boardman Fire Department which assured adequate communications during a hospital emergency as required by the fire codes.
- Fire Prevention Officers, over a series of years, provided guidance to the builders of The Beeghly Medical Complex to ensure they complied with Boardman's fire codes during construction. Beeghly became a major medical complex in Boardman.
- Fire Prevention Officers provided the best fire safety instructions to grade school children by acquiring fire Safety Trailers through Federal Grants.
- Fire Prevention developed a Gas Well Program. They located and mapped the locations of all gas well heads. They established rules and regulations for gas well companies to follow when drilling new wells providing for safe and secure locations.
- They spearheaded a mission to identify neighborhood streets that were too narrow to allow cars to park on both sides of the street. They successfully lobbied the Trustees to limit parking to one side only on those narrow streets and to have "NO PARKING" signs installed.
- They required plan reviews of all new construction prior to the start of new projects. They could add fire safety requirements that the builders were expected to adhere to.
- They provide fire extinguisher classes for employees of many businesses throughout Boardman. The training extended to teaching seniors in high school to use a fire extinguisher.
- A program was developed whereby a business could buy a Knox Box from the fire department and secure it to the outside of their building. This box was used to store keys for entry into the building at the time of a fire alarm or smoke in the building. This helped prevent unnecessary damage to doors or windows when the fire department was trying to gain entry to check for a fire.
- In 2010, the Fire Prevention Office led by Lieutenant Jim McCreary proposed to the Trustees the fire department adopt the International Fire Codes, (IFC). These codes contained additional regulations to safeguard life and property from fires and explosion hazards. The Trustees approved the request and adopted the new fire codes.

Firefighter's Local 1176

Before 1918, many local firefighter unions joined the AFL-CIO for representation. With a need for an organization dedicated to serving the interests of firefighters, the International Association of Fire Fighters was founded on February 28, 1918. It was organized to unite firefighters for better wages and improved safety. There was a time when firefighters worked seven days a week, had few benefits and safety meant putting a wet towel over your face before running into flames. By 1939, the IAFF celebrated the spread of civil service laws, a significant shortening of hours worked, and growing salaries for firefighters. That year also marked the IAFF's first efforts involving occupational safety.

In the fifties, if you were a paid fire department of over 8 firefighters, you were expected to join the IAFF. It is within this time frame that Boardman Fire Department started to employ more full-time firefighters.

If a fire department was going to benefit from the support of the IAFF to negotiate for improved benefits, they had to do it as a member of the International Association. So, with that in mind, Chief Gifford, with the support of the few paid members of the Boardman Fire Department, also with the help of IAFF Local 312 from the Youngstown Fire Department, joined the IAFF. To meet the minimum requirement of 8 firefighters on the department, the Chief enlisted some of the volunteer firemen to also join the union. This enabled them to meet the membership requirement.

On October 25, 1954, Dan Eberhart, Vice President of the Ohio Firefighters Organization, presented the National Charter to President Larry Nordquist of the new IAFF Boardman Firefighters Local 1176. The Vice President was Wayne Ewing and the Secretary/Treasurer was Don Neapolitan.

Vindicator file photo/ October 26, 1954 | Members of the Boardman Fire Department pose with a certificate of affiliation with the International Association of Fire Fighters. They are, from left, A.R. Neapolitan, William Skinner, Jack Beck, Lawrence Nordquist, assistant chief and president of the local; Don Neapolitan, secretary; Dan Eberhardt, vice president of the Ohio Association of Fire Fighters; M.W. Gifford, chief, and Wayne Ewing, vice president.

On August 1, 1955, Barney Davison was appointed to the fire department as a full-time firefighter. He joined the union in 1957. I asked him why he had not joined the union in 1955 and he said that Chief Gifford and Assistant Chief Nordquist decided that he should not join right away, that it was not proper. Two years later, Wayne Ewing asked him if he would like to join. Davison said that guys were dropping out of the union because some of the initial members were volunteer firefighters. This was a problem because the volunteers had different needs than the paid firefighters plus they belonged to the union at the mill and there was pressure on them not to belong to two different unions.

He remembers that his dues were about $6 per month. Davison said that there were no written contracts, they would negotiate an issue, settle it, and agree to it on a verbal commitment from the Trustees. Of the three Trustees, he said Harold Perkins was more sympathetic to their issues as he was in the union at the mill. He said that Trustees Mansell and Heintzelman were more difficult to negotiate with. Negotiation attempts were more successful on some items than others. They benefited from improvements in the Widows and Orphans Fund, Kelley Days, and uniform purchase compensation. When it came to wages, vacations, and holidays, the Trustees took more of a "take it or leave it" position. But they did make some improvements through their negotiating and they had the means to plead their case when something unusual came up. Once when a child was drowning in Mill Creek Park, Boardman Fire Department had divers at the scene and there was a need for numerous volunteer helpers. Many of the firefighters took time off from their part-time jobs to help with the effort. Local 1176 went to the Trustees and successfully negotiated partial compensation for the men who lost wages by being absent from their part-time jobs. Davison remembers that Dan Eberhart provided help to Local 1176 whenever they needed it and was a tremendous help in guiding the firefighters in establishing the union.

This document records the first meeting of Boardman Firefighters Local 1176.

The first meeting was held on Oct. 25, 1954 in Br. Neapolitan's cellar. Br. Dan Eberhart of Local 312 also Vice-president of the Ohio 6th District was also present. the National Charter was presented ~~for~~ by Br. Eberhart; he, then swore the members in. Imidetly following he swore in the Local officers. Pres. Lawrence Nordquist; Vice-President Wayne Ewing and Sec.-Treas.- Don Neapolitan.

Br. Eberhart discussed the functions that the National does. Next he told us about certain legislature in the state, [illegible] present.

With that the meeting was adjorned

Fraternally yours.

Donald N. Neapolitan
Sec-Treas.

Based on the next document, Boardman was re-affiliating with the IAFF. As it turned out, there was a problem with the qualifications of some of the men who had previously joined Local 1176, so the national affiliation was rescinded. This document records a meeting held on May 31, 1957, by the firefighters and addresses how they could regain their affiliation with the International Firefighters. The meeting minutes identify previous members as Gifford, Nordquist, and Ewing. The new members who joined the union were Bush, deSaulles, R. Ewing, and Davison to total 7 members.

May 31, 1957

A meeting was held at #2 fire station to discuss re-affiliation of the local with both the International and Ohio association. Brother Dan Eberhardt, Youngstown Local 312 and Vice Pres. of the Ohio 6th District, met with us and explained the terms by which we could rejoin the associations. The old members, Bros. Gifford, Nordquist and W. Ewing were to pay International Per-Capita tax back to March 1957. The new members, Bros. Bush, de Saulles, R. Ewing, and Davison were required to pay only initiation fee and dues for June. The Ohio Assoc. required no back Per-Capita tax from anyone. The members present agreed to these terms and all money due was given to Bro. Eberhardt to send to the association.

New officers are J. de Saulles President and W. Ewing, Sec-Treas.

Absent from meeting were J. de Saulles and S. Nordquist.

Meeting adjourned at 9:00 PM.

Wayne Ewing

Sec.-Treas.

Bob Reno was appointed as a full-time firefighter in 1965. He said that he joined the firefighter's union at the earliest opportunity. He felt that labor relations with the administration were very poor during the first two years he was on the department. Eventually, he ran for union President and won. Reno said, "As the union President, I worked with Dan Eberhart and Rocco Russo from Youngstown. They provided us with a lot of help. I was able to get the 72-hour work week reduced to a 56-hour work week. In 1967, we had a campaign where we went to the Trustee's houses constantly and lobbied them to give us the reduction in the work week and eventually they gave in." Reno said "The biggest issue over the years was wages. There was a time when we had equal pay with the police. We lost that and tried at, each contract negotiation, to get it back. The other issue that I am proud of is that I was able to get us longevity pay for every two years of service up to 10 years."

The history of Boardman Firefighters Local 1176 would not be complete without the biographical information about one of the strongest forces for change that the department had experienced, Steve Hierro. Steve said to me, "I know that I can be a pain in the rear," But most firefighters would have to agree that the firefighters benefited from his determination which led to so many contractual improvements in benefits and working conditions.

Hierro joined the fire department full-time on July 1, 1965. He chose the profession of firefighter because he previously served in fire protection in the Air Force. He joined the Air Force in 1953 and spent four years on active duty. He was placed in fire protection directly from basic training. While in the Air Force, he experienced structure fires but the larger fires were in big airplanes. The worst fire he experienced was with a B-47 Bomber. It had crashed into a munitions bunker causing a major fire. After active duty, Steve remained with the Air Force Reserves for another 30 years. He retired from the Air Force after 34 ½ years as a Master Sargent.

Because of his firefighting experience, Hierro joined the Boardman Volunteer Firefighters around 1963. In 1965, he took advantage of an opportunity to join the department full-time. He earned his State of Ohio Firefighter 120 hour training certificate quickly. He didn't serve much time on probation because he had brought with him his Air Force experience and because of his time as a Boardman volunteer firefighter. Steve describes his first year on the department as a nightmare. He was assigned to work Number 3 Station at Lockwood and Shields Road and often worked alone. His objection was partly due to the loneliness of working by himself and in part because he felt it was dangerous to respond to a fire with only one person. Steve worked all of the fire stations but spent most of his early years at Number 3 Station. The truck assigned to Number 3 Station was the '41 Mack.

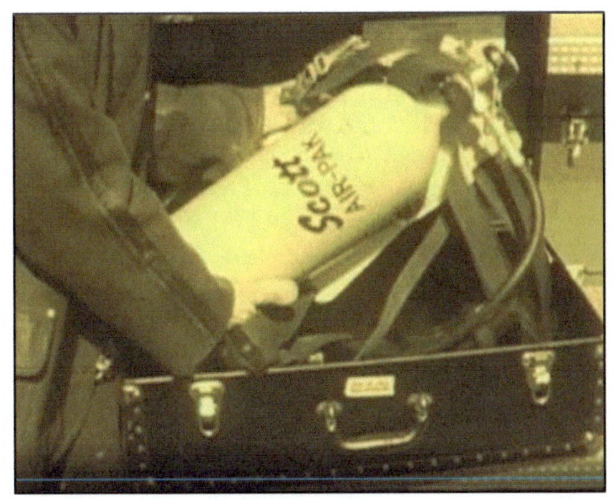

When asked about innovations in the fire service, he described the first tool the department purchased to assist with vehicle rescues; the Hydraulic Porta Power Rescue Tool. This was a hydraulic spreading tool used to pry open doors and move smashed metal. The hydraulic spreaders only moved when the operator pumped the handle to activate the spread. This was followed, years later, by the Hurst Rescue tools which did the same operation but it was done automatically with the push of a trigger and had much more power. Steve also points out that he was able to receive a donation of a pair of discarded parachute harnesses from the Air Force. These were configured to help remove a trapped person from a hole or a well. He was also able to introduce to the department a silver protective suit that would shield the wearer from direct flame.

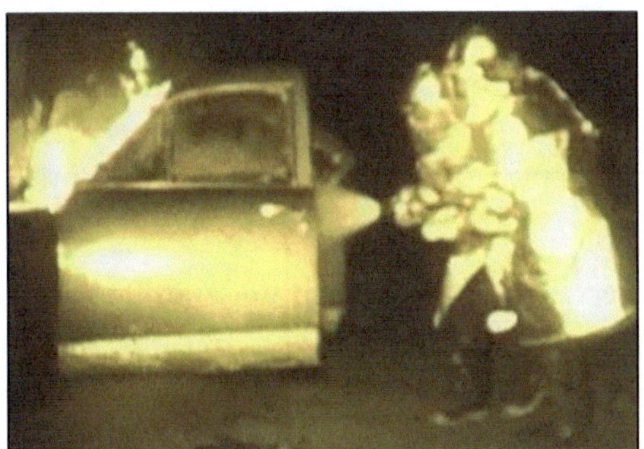

He remembers some of the bigger fires such as D. D. Davis Construction, the Boardman Plaza fire, Scotsford Volkswagen, and the day Randall Good died when his car was bombed which set fire to his apartment complex. Hierro said, "He was the pump engineer on most fires."

Hierro said that the mood of the fire department when he joined was not great when it came to relations with the officers. He said that there was no give and take. There was no room for discussion with the officers who wouldn't allow any input from the firefighters. He said he was raised in a union house. His father was a strong union man from the mill and he was raised to believe that all working conditions were subject to give and take discussion. When he joined the fire department full-time, there were a total of 15 men on the department and all of them were in the union. Hierro joined the union within his first month on the department. He said the firefighters were not happy with the employee/administration relationship but they had to go along as they did not have the means to negotiate improvements. The administration viewed the union as strictly a social club and did not respect them as legitimate representatives of the labor force. They did not feel they had to negotiate with them.

Firemen Have Plan To Solve Dilemma

Boardman Firefighters Association, Local 1176 AFL-CIO, will present a plan, May 15 to the Boardman Township Trustees that will enable them to have a 56-hour work week instead of 72 without hiring additional men or closing any of the Boardman fire stations.

Steve Hierro, vice president of the local, states that Boardman has modern up-to-date fire stations including training and equipment and are only "behind the time in the hourly work week."

Robert J. Reno, president, told the trustees at a recent meeting that Youngstown has a 56-hour week and Campbell a 40-hour week.

Reno said that at the recent meeting the trustees were told that the state fire-fighters is advocating a bill in the state legislature that would make a 56-hour week for firemen mandatory. They were told that eight men would be laid off if this bill passed, Reno said.

In the State of Ohio 91% of the fire departments work a 56-hour work week, 6¼% work a 60-hour work week and 2 6/10% work a 72-hour work week.

The firemen are convinced that if their plan is accepted it will work to the benefit

(continued to page 2)

There were a lot of issues big and small nagging the firefighters. Some were very mundane. One of the items that bothered the men went as follows: during the day, you wore a basic work uniform. At 7:00 PM, you were required to change into your fire department dress uniform clothes (minus the dress coat). If there was a Trustees meeting at Number 1 Station, then you must also wear a tie until the meeting is done.

Hierro said, "He never really participated in the union leadership, but when Bob Reno decided, in 1968, that he no longer wanted to serve as the President, he said he would run for it." And then Hierro spent over a decade as the President of Local 1176.

Over the years, not all Boardman firefighters belonged to the union. When I joined the fire department in 1972, there were only 6 men in the union out of 25 firefighters on the department. They were Steve Hierro, Bob Reno, Dick Schneider, Herb Inman, Gerry Felger, Bill Manley Sr. As the next few years went by, the firefighters became disgruntled with their inability to make meaningful improvements to their benefits. Also, there were issues with how promotions were handled which brought Civil Service to the table.

Issues were frequently taken to Chief Cover but nothing would get resolved. Boardman police officers were also feeling the same dissatisfaction with labor relations.

In 1970 Democrats Tom Carney and Bob Bannon were both elected as Trustees. The change in the administration tilting towards the Democrats made a difference, for union members. Then, in 1973, Tom Carney won a seat in the State House of Representatives and subsequently resigned from his Trustee position. While in the State Legislature, he worked on a bill to allow Townships with a population over 10,000 to implement Civil Service for their employees. Carney said that he tailor-made the bill for Boardman Township. He thought Boardman should be on par with other communities.

Civil Service was a big issue for the firefighters who did not agree that the Fire Chief should be permitted to promote any firefighter he chose, ignoring the tradition of promoting the next senior man.

Shortly after Carney passed the Civil Service bill, he introduced a bill to permit Townships to appoint an Administrator. This bill was also passed. Boardman Trustees quickly appointed Bob Schaal as the first Township Administrator.

Yellow Trend, Sleeping Blankets and Civil Service was the headline of the Boardman News following a meeting with the Trustees and about 30 members of Boardman Fire Department, held Tuesday, October 19, 1976. Union members sensing a shift in the mood of the Trustees to discuss topics of interest to the fire department put together a wish list of improvements they hoped could be made to working conditions and benefits. This list was presented to the Trustees, in a special meeting that was open to the public. The list included; changing the fire truck, bunker coat, and helmet color to yellow for better visibility, flexibility in wearing work clothes vs. dress clothing, issuing a blanket to each man vs. sharing blankets with multiple people, wearing a badge on our shirt at all times, allow two men on vacation at the same time, buying groceries while on duty, able to visit home for Thanksgiving and Christmas dinners, revise promotion policy, permit a lunchtime nap, a 6% pay raise, add a fire prevention officer, make improvements to living conditions in the fire stations and more.

This bold step, by the firefighters, to take this long list of requests directly to the Trustees was fiercely debated by the department officers and the local press. Chief Cover was resistant to most issues since they affected the fire department budget. In the end, Trustees approved some of the firefighter's recommendations such as fire coats helmet colors, and blankets, and many requests were viewed favorably subject to budget constraints. But regardless of the outcome, this positive exchange of ideas opened the door to the future of labor negotiations. This specific episode paved the way for the implementation of Civil Service and recognition of Local 1176 as the bargaining agent for the firefighters and a written labor agreement.

Hierro and police officer Dick Sell testified before Carney's House of Representatives Committee on Civil Service. In February of 1978, the Trustees voted to place Police and Fire department employees under Civil Service status for hiring, promotions, and discipline resolution. This was followed, two months later, with the Trustee recognizing the bargaining units for both the firefighters and police officers. Contract negotiations followed. Hierro said, "After the collective bargaining agreement was signed, relations with the administration settled down. Local 1176 used the contracts of other fire departments in Ohio with similar populations and department sizes as a template for their first contract. Finally, the Township became a Civil Service Township and the Boardman Trustees recognized both the fire and police unions as bargaining agents for their membership.

This notice was sent from Township Clerk-Treasurer Genevieve Novicky that the Trustees had recognized Local 1176 as the bargaining agent for the firefighters.

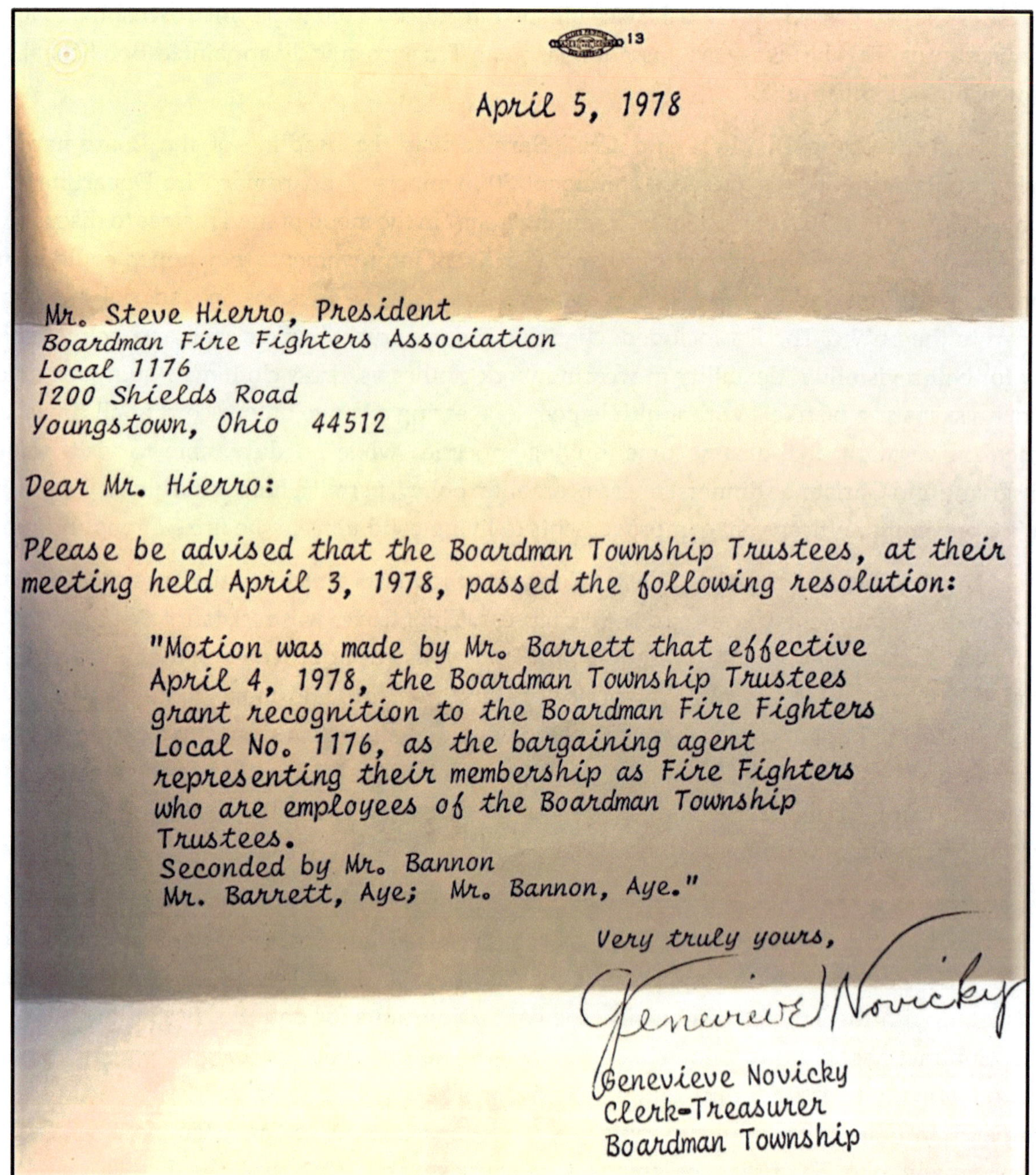
April 5, 1978

Mr. Steve Hierro, President
Boardman Fire Fighters Association
Local 1176
1200 Shields Road
Youngstown, Ohio 44512

Dear Mr. Hierro:

Please be advised that the Boardman Township Trustees, at their meeting held April 3, 1978, passed the following resolution:

> "Motion was made by Mr. Barrett that effective April 4, 1978, the Boardman Township Trustees grant recognition to the Boardman Fire Fighters Local No. 1176, as the bargaining agent representing their membership as Fire Fighters who are employees of the Boardman Township Trustees.
> Seconded by Mr. Bannon
> Mr. Barrett, Aye; Mr. Bannon, Aye."

Very truly yours,

Genevieve Novicky

Genevieve Novicky
Clerk-Treasurer
Boardman Township

There was a great difference between the Trustees talking with the firefighters in 1954 leading to a verbal agreement to grant benefit improvements versus agreeing to recognize Local 1176 as the bargaining agent for the firefighters and signing a written contract. The firefighters had finally achieved security in maintaining benefits and had a mechanism to negotiate future improvements.

First Contract for Local 1176

On December 4, 1978, President Steve Hierro, Vice President Joe Ignazio, and Secretary/Treasurer Jim Dorman signed the first bargaining agreement with Boardman Township Trustees. The first contract was called a Memorandum Of Understanding but it was a contract. Assisting the union negotiating team was Dan Eberhart, Vice President of the Ohio Firefighters Organization. This first contract took weeks and weeks of tough negotiations to achieve a document that both the Township and the firefighters were happy with. The contract consisted of 25 Articles that laid out work rules and fringe benefit items. The highlights of this agreement include:

- Article 2. Recognition- Local 1176 is recognized as the bargaining agent for all sworn and uniformed employees of the fire department.
- Article 7. Grievance Procedure- This section first defines a grievance as a failure of the Township to comply with the law or provisions of the agreement. The procedures to file a grievance were listed.
- Article 10. Overtime- Overtime will be paid out at one and one-half times the basic hourly rate of pay of the employee.
- Article 11. Temporary Assignments- This specifies that a firefighter may be assigned to work in the absence of a person in a higher rank and will be paid the rate of pay of the higher rank.
- Article 12. Sick Leave- Lays out the rate sick leave is earned, how it is to be used, and how an employee will be reimbursed for accumulated sick leave upon retirement.
- Article 14. Vacations- Specified the amount of vacation earned for years of employment. The benefit states that the firefighter earned; 2 weeks after 1 year of service, 3 weeks after 6 years, 4 weeks after 13 years, and 5 weeks after 23 years.
- Article 15. Holidays- Holidays will be per the Ohio Revised Code.
- Article 18. Wages and Salaries- starting firefighter $11,616, 5-year firefighter $13,535, Fire Prevention $14,315, Captain $14,801, Assistant Chief $16,082.
- Article 22. No Strike or Lock Out Clause- Firefighters agree not to go on strike at any time.
- Article 25 Terms of Agreement- The firefighters agreed to a three-year contract with a wage reopener agreement after one year.

The firefighters would have preferred a shorter term of the agreement, but Township Administrator Bob Schaal stood his ground making the three-year provision mandatory if a contract agreement were to be reached! The firefighters reluctantly accepted this to achieve signing the first contract.

Over the years, there have been many changes in the bargaining agreements. The firefighters achieved many significant gains and the Township elicited concessions in areas the union regretted granting in earlier contracts. Negotiations are all about give and take. The provisions in the articles are bargaining chips during negotiations.

PD,FD Bargaining Units Recognized

4-6-78

Boardman Township Trustees opened a new relationship with employees of the police and fire departments on Monday night when bargaining agents for both groups were recognized; the Fraternal Order of Police, Lodge 43 and chapter 1176 of the International Association of Firefighters.

The FOP lodged was organized in 1972 and shortly thereafter began seeking recognition while the firemen's group has been trying since 1958 to gain bargaining recognition.

FOP president is George Statler while Steve Hierro head the firemen's local.

Next step in the recognition process will be for both groups to sit down with Trustees Robert Bannon, William Houser and Thomas Barrett and work out a memorandum of understanding.

According to Hierro, the firemen will model their memorandum after the Liberty Township firemen's local. Such a memorandum was turned over to Trustees in December Hierro said, adding "We expect we'll get some of the items and others we won't get."

The FOP was supposed to have submitted their memorandum of understanding to Trustees on Tuesday.

Both memorandums are supposed to deal with general working conditions, clothing allowances, vacation policy, longevity and hospitalization.

An FOP member told the Boardman News that group would also seek to negotiate a salary item in their memorandum.

In approving the recognition on Monday night, Bannon said "that's all" Trustees did, recognize the bargaining units. "We'll go from there," he added.

No dates or times have been established for the respective groups to sit down across the table.

In other action on Monday night fire chief Don Cover noted work has slowed on the renovation of the number one fire station on Boardman-Poland Rd.

"Indications were the work was supposed to have been completed by Mar. 1. Although the work isn't yet finished, it's not causing any particular problems," Cover said.

Outside work and installation of a main water line are two items yet to be completed on the fire station.

The contract had been in place for only one year and it seemed like bargaining issues had just been settled when it was time to start all over again on wages. Hierro admits that although wage improvements had been generous by any standard, the firefighters were not on equal footing with peer fire departments. Even though raises had been in the 9% and 10% range in past years, firefighters wanted even bigger increases to reach parity with other community's firefighters. Our firefighters were not satisfied with what the Trustees were offering in the new contract and chose to picket and take their case to the public. (I was a member of Local 1176 Executive Committee at the time and supported the picketing.) On October 29, 1979, the firefighters found themselves performing informational picketing at the main fire station. They were prepared to walk the Boardman neighborhoods and pass out thousands of flyers, to try to persuade the residents to support the firefighters. The flyers never made it out of the boxes, but the pressure brought the Trustees back to the table. The Trustees added non-salary perks to the written agreement to appease the firefighters.

FIREMEN GO PUBLIC — Contending that their pay is too low and that township offers for raises don't go far enough, Boardman Fire Fighters Local 1176 set up informational pickets this morning to notify the public of their plight. They stressed that their action in no way obstructs departmental work with only off-duty firemen in the demonstration. Leaders of other area labor unions joined them this morning. The firemen have rejected a nine percent hike on a one-year contract which would bring the base pay to $14,700.

I asked Steve Hierro how satisfied he was with the accomplishments of Local 1176 over the years he had served as the President. He said, "I was 100% satisfied. You can't achieve everything you want but we made significant improvements in wages, benefits, working conditions, and safety to make the efforts worthwhile." One of the union's biggest accomplishments occurred in June of 1967 while Bob Reno was President. The work week changed from 72 hours to a 56-hour work week. The Trustees had to put up with a storm of firefighters' wives who attended a Trustee's meeting and spoke about the harm to their families with their husbands missing from home for so many hours.

I worked with Steve Hierro on the first contracts, writing many of the articles as the union secretary. I found him to be tenacious, relentless, a person who never gave up because he felt he was right, a genuine pain in the neck of the Chief and Administration, but above all else, he never gave up trying to improve our financial position and our safety conditions.

Mike Walsh joined Boardman Fire Department on December 16, 1990, and retired on March 21, 2020. "I took over the office of President, from Steve Hierro on January 1, 1995. I give Steve a lot of credit for how he dealt with Administrators and Trustees over the years. He gained a lot of ground in our contract while he was in the office. When I ran for President, the younger guys were looking for benefits that suited them and Steve was looking down the road to provide benefits to the older guys who were getting ready to retire. There was a lot of divisiveness in the ranks. Several guys were pushing me to run. When I decided to throw my hat in the ring, I thought I could bring the guys back together and find common ground on how to improve our benefits. I started holding Christmas parties to improve camaraderie, to get people together and realize we are just a big family."

"I was fairly new with the department, with only four years seniority, when I became union President. I was learning as I went and I did find it to be a little overwhelming. But I always tried to find a compromise with management over issues with which we disagreed ."

"In the years that I was President, we got a pretty good contract for the firefighters. We had been trying to achieve pay parity with the police for years. Finally, we did achieve parity with the police patrol officers and the firefighters. It took a lot of work on my part to get that done. Sometimes, I stayed up all night and had paperwork scattered all around my kitchen to organize my presentation."

"We achieved bidding on fire stations during my time in office. Firefighters were able to bid for a new opening at fire stations by seniority."

"It took a lawsuit but I was able to achieve a change in how FLSA (Fair Labor Standards Act) money was distributed. We were able to gain the FLSA money at the time we earned it rather than waiting until close to retirement before we started to see the money."

Jim Hoover, on January 1, 2002, Hoover was elected President of the firefighter's union, Local 1176. He decided to run for President because he wanted to try a different approach to handling the union's affairs. He wanted to give his ideas a try. He said, "I was very EMS minded and the International Association of Fire Fighters was preaching fire-based EMS and I thought we could do a better job with that as a goal."

"While I was still President, Chris Pater, Rob John, Tom Roberts, and I put together a presentation about improving staffing. We were in the Trustee's conference room with the Trustees. After the presentation, I thought we were on the same page in agreeing that improvements could be made in staffing and the money seemed to be there. We had the Tri-Data study supporting our call for improvements. The Trustees committed and eventually brought our staffing up to forty three firefighters which was a huge step." This provided 13 firefighters per shift, 3 Fire Prevention Officers, and 1 Fire Chief.

"Overall, as President, I felt I kept us afloat without too many wars. I tried to do things to improve our image."

Harry Wolfe said, "I came from a union family." Wolfe became a member of Local 1176, the firefighter's union. After being with the union for a while, he became a member of the grievance committee and later the recording secretary. Eventually, he ran for and was voted in as union President on January 1, 2008. Wolfe said, " I always wanted to be the person to stand up for other people." Wolfe became President and held the position for nine years. He took a break for one year and then held the position for one more year.

Wolfe remembered, "Shortly after I became union President, Chief Dorman called me into his office and said we have a fiscal emergency and we would have to be laying off firefighters. From that point on, it was the battle. This is why I stayed union President as long as I did. The department was under attack in a way that I never thought was possible."

Wolfe said, "I reached out to the State (of Ohio union officials) and the IAFF (International Association of Fire Fighters) for help. Many firefighters from all over Ohio came here." Wolfe continued indignantly, "For this, they called us union thugs. Decisions were being made that affected the lives of the firefighters and people were offended when our guys called in other people to help us show unity! Those people were here to say if it's important to Boardman, it's important to our community too."

I asked Wolfe to name one big thing he accomplished as a union President and he said, "During that difficult time, we were able to get the Safety Forces Levy passed immediately." Wolfe was his proudest when he talked about getting firefighters' jobs back! "We were also able to get six of the nine firefighters back. And we were able to get the layoff recall extended from three years to five years. This provision helped the three firefighters, still laid off, to be offered their jobs back."

Scott Murray said, "I ran for the office of President because I wanted to try to take a different approach in dealing with the Chief and the Trustees." He became President on January 1, 2018. "While I was President, I handled issues and grievances as they came. I felt I was conservative in how I handled issues. I think I understood the business owners' aspect of issues. It takes money to pay the guys but if the funds aren't there then we have to figure something else out. Most guys have only experienced one side of life, the employee's side of life. The following year, Harry decided to run for reelection and won."

Murray said he was disappointed that, "In the past, negotiations were handled by the Township Administrator, the Fire Chief, and the Union negotiators. Now we have attorneys for both union and management arguing for issues for their side."

Brian Halquist joined Boardman Fire Department in 2018. He became President on January 1, 2020. In November of 2022, he had been the Local 1176 President for three years. He said, "The most significant event that had happened in recent years had to do with improving the starting salary for new hires. Eleven years ago, the starting salary was $37,000 but it had gotten knocked down to $24,000.00. We seem to be just a training ground for new firefighters. In the five years I have been here, I already have fifteen people under me with less seniority. That's from retirements and people coming and going to different departments. We hope to get the starting salary back to a point where firefighters stay here rather than look elsewhere for a better salary."

The past contract negotiations were tough. Both management and union used labor attorneys. But we feel good because, at the end of negotiations, we got about $500,000 put into our contract from a third party fact finder. We got a couple of steps knocked off of base salary increases. Also, the new firefighters received a 1% increase more than the older guys. We are just now getting back to a $37,000 starting salary. We hope to get back to where firefighters are happy to stay because they are satisfied with the pay. Overall, the gain from those items has a value of about $500,000 to the whole membership over 3 years. Now we are working on healthcare cost improvements.

IAFF Local 1176 Presidents

Over the years, many men have served as the President of Boardman Firefighters Local 1176. They were persistent in their efforts to provide good working conditions for the firefighters, fair and livable salaries, and benefits for the firefighters and their families. These men worked hard to make sure the people who had chosen to do this dangerous job were compensated for the sacrifices that they made.

- October 1, 1954 Lawrence Nordquist
- May 31, 1957 J. B. deSaulles
- January 1, 1959 Bill Bush
- October 8, 1959 Barney Davison
- January 1, 1962 Charlie Tomalka
- January 1, 1966 Dick Schneider
- January 1, 1967 Bob Reno
- January 1, 1968 Steve Hierro
- January 1, 1969 J. B. deSaulles
- January 13, 1969 Bill Elmo
- September 30, 1969 Francis Buckley
- January 1, 1970 Bob Reno
- September 25, 1970 Steve Hierro
- March 2, 1971 Bob Reno
- January 1, 1972 John Campbell
- January 1, 1974 Steve Hierro
- January 1, 1981 Keith Hamilton
- January 1, 1984 Steve Hierro
- January 1, 1987 Jim Wilson Resigned January 23, 1987 and appointed Chief
- January 23, 1987 Ken Pahon
- January 1, 1988 Steve Hierro
- January 1, 1995 Mike Walsh
- January 1, 2002 Jim Hoover
- January 1, 2008 Harry Wolfe
- January 1, 2018 Scott Murray
- January 1, 2019 Harry Wolfe
- January 1, 2020 Brian Hallquist

The longest serving President was Steve Hierro with fifteen years and five months. The second longest serving President was Harry Wolfe with eleven years.

Full Time and Volunteer Firefighters

The following pages include a list of every full-time and volunteer firefighter that could be found in the fire department records and archives. There are 377 names on the list. Next to each name is the date that he or she joined the fire department. Some start dates could not be found.

Alexander, Bert	1926
Alexander, Melvin	1937
Allen, Reade	2001
Alman, Jack	1938
Altdoeffer	1935
Amero, Bill	
Amon, Dave	1963
Anstrom, James	1938
Applegate, Bill	1968
Ariza, Rob	1999
Austin, James	1939
Bailey, Brock	2012
Bair, Leo	1927
Baldwin, Bill	1951
Barber, Brian	1996
Barber, Tom	
Bartelli, Reverand	1959
Bayless, Bob	1966
Bayne, Robert	1954
Bayus, Ray	1968
Beck, Jack	1952
Becker, Rick	1970
Beede, Paul	1925
Begalla, Steve	1991
Bender, Ralph	1937
Berardi, John	1998
Betts, Robert	1949
Black, Chet	1923
Black, Dudley	1929
Black, Fred	1926
Bletzer, Bud	1942
Bloom, Kevin	2005
Bobola, Tom	1971
Bohn, George	1926
Bonser, Bob	1961
Elser, Otto	
Boyer, Steve	
Brooks, C.H.	1926
Brown, Alexander	1954
Brown, George	2011
Brown, Larry	1939
Bruner Robert	2022
Bruno, Greg	
Bucheit, Pete	1953
Buckley, Chuck	2001
Buckley, Francis	1965
Burkell, Chuck	1973
Burkhert, Fred	1966
Burrier, George	1940
Bush, Bill	1954
Caltumo, Harry	
Campbell, John	1961
Candella, Steve	1956
Candor, Mark	1988
Carlson, Chester	1929
Carlson, Dave	1970
Carlson, Kermit	1925
Carlson, Quinton	1926
Carter, Harlely	1958
Cartwright, Ed	1941
Cartwright, Paul	1940
Caskey, Reverand	1955
Catherman, James	1941
Catherman, Paul	1926
Cencia, Dino	
Centrello, J.	1955
Centrello, V.	1955
Chambers, Bill	1926
Cichon, Tom	1991
Clause, Robert	1950
Cleeveley, Bob	1965
Elswick, Jordan	2022
Clemmons, Paul	1926
Coler, Park	1926
Comm, Bud	1965
Comstock, Chip	1988
Conroy, Shaun	2013
Cover, Dave	1966
Cover, Don	1943
Crawford, Ken	1969
Creed, Leo	1937
Creps, Jack	1944
Creps, Tom	1950
D'Apolito, Steve	1978
Davis, Bales	1927
Davis, Bob	1970
Davis, Don	1939
Davis, Myron	1926
Davison, Alfred (Barney)	1955
DelBoccio, Ed	1991
Delozier, Jack	1954
deSaulles, J. B.	1955
deSaulles, Jack	1938
Dicks, Ken	1988
Dilley, Ed	1926
Divelbliss, Howard	1955
Donadee, Tom	1995
Dorman, Dick	1966
Dorman, Jim	1968
Drummond, Tim	1985
Dubic, Steve	2005
Duke, Harry	1926
Dundon, Tom	1953
Dustman, Frank	1926
Dustman, Paul	1927
Eckman, H. M.	1923
Elmo, Bill	1964
Erickson, Ray	1937

Evans, Bill	1967	Heintzelman, Ken	1926	Kyle, Howard	1923
Ewing, Harold (Bus)	1952	Heintzelmlan, William	1959	LaBelle, Fred	1937
Ewing, Robert	1951	Hemphill, Gary	2003	Lewis, Dan	1970
Ewing, Wayne	1954	Henderson, A. L.	1926	Lewis, Jon	2001
Felger, Gerry	1965	Henderson, Dave	1938	Lockeic, Conrad	1976
Ferrando, Will	2012	Hermesdorf, Tim		Lodge, Kevin	
Finamore, Brandon	2022	Hernan, Ken		Lundquist, Charles Rev	1956
Fink, Bob	1956	Herubin, Chris	1992	Lyons, Mike	2000
Flemming, Bill		Hidinger, Eugene	1937	Machingo, Matt	2019
Flynn, Chris	1998	Hierro, Steve	1965	Manley, Bill Jr.	1980
Ford, Sam	1926	Hinderliter, Cory	2016	Manley, Bill Sr.	1957
Gallimore, Jeff	2003	Holl, Homer	1923	Marenkovic, Jim	1994
Gardner, Jay		Hollquist, Brian	2018	Marsh, John Jr.	1965
Garland, Mike	2004	Holmes, Bob	1937	Mauch, Don	1975
Garris, Andrew	2019	Hoover, Fred	1965	May, Kathy	1992
Gartner, Bob	1965	Hoover, Jim	1995	Mayberry, Eugene	1948
Gebharadt, Austin	2018	Horning, Chris	2004	Mayo, Rick	
Geise, Harry	1926	Houser, Gary	1975	McAllister, Paul	1958
Gibson, Ed	1961	Houston, Fred	1953	McBurney, Eric	
Gifford, L.	1959	Huston, W.	1955	McCartney, Nate	2021
Gifford, Merle	1923	Hutchison, Jonathan	2019	McCloud, Tom	1989
Gilmore, Brandon	2021	Ignazio, Joe	1975	McCreary, Jim	1991
Gilmour, Erin	2017	Inglis, Robert	1965	McIntosh, Bill	1937
Glaser, Bill	2001	Inman, Herb	1961	McLane, W.	1954
Gluck, Norm	1927	Jack, Paul	1923	Meek, Charles	1923
Gongaware, Carl	1942	Jacobson, Richard	1950	Mesmer, Vern	1961
Grande, Gloria	2001	Jarvis, John	1998	Messmer, Frank	1937
Grossman, Mike	1975	Jenkins, Ivor	1956	Miller, Nathan	2015
Guerrieri, Adam	2005	Jessop, Howard	1931	Moore, Maynard	
Gulgas, John	2004	John, Rob	1999	Moorhead, Mark	1974
Gustafson, Carl	1954	Johns, Harry		Moran, G.	1959
Haire, Troy	2015	Johnston, Lou	1963	Moreland, Dewey	1949
Hamilton, Keith	1973	Jones, Clark	1972	Morgan, Brian	2000
Hanlin, Scott	2004	Jones, H. W.	1926	Morgan, Gary	1986
Hanna, Albert	1937	Jones, Tom		Morgan, Harry	1943
Hanna, Bill	1950	Jordan, Frank	1991	Murray, Ian	2021
Hanna, Dave	1950	Junge, W.	1938	Murray, Scot	2002
Harrison, Joseph Rev	1970	Kennedy, John Rev	1961	Musser, L.	1951
Haun, Jim		Kennedy, Todd	1996	Neapolitan, Andy (Red)	1936
Heaven, Blaine	1956	Kibler, Phil	1966	Neapolitan, Billy	1953
Heaven, Ron	1956	Kibler, Phil Jr.		Neapolitan, Bob	1949
Heaver, Andy	1968	Kloes, Don	1991	Neapolitan, Don	1953
Heckman, Stanley	1938	Kollmorgen, Jessica	2012	Newman, Sabrina	1998
Heintzelman, Fay	1923	Komandt, Paul	2013	Nockowski, Eric	2015
Heintzelman, John	1926	Kummer, J.	1964	Nordquist, Clarence	1926

Name	Year
Nordquist, Dale	1989
Nordquist, Lawrence	1926
Nordquist, Sig	1926
Northrup, Harry	1941
O'Hara, Brandon	2019
Osborne, Jason	2009
Osborne, Russ	1986
Pahon, Ken	1978
Park, Jonathan	2016
Parker, Bill	1943
Parker, Roy	1929
Parks, Earl	1944
Parry, Doctor Robert	1963
Pater, Chris	1999
Patrick, Bob	2014
Paulin, Everett	1950
Pawlosky, John	1977
Peppel, Brian	1987
Perry, Steve	1949
Phillips, Ryan	2022
Phillips, Cliff	2003
Pitzer, Mark	2003
Poole, Ben	2013
Powell, Frank	1928
Powell, P.	1948
Powell, Paul	1937
Price, Charles	1963
Price, Rick	
Pugh, Bob (Butch)	1956
Pulley, Bob	1966
Quentin, James	1938
Rappach, Shawn	2003
Rauch, John	
Rauschenbauck, Robert	
Rauschenberg, Rick	
Reade, Allen	2001
Reader, Mark	1985
Reebel, Tony	1971
Reed, Frank	1929
Reed, Paul	1927
Reese, Jerry	
Reinthaler, Dom	2021
Reiter, Anthony	2013
Reno, Bob	1965
Rhodes, Gene	1965
Riley, Mike	1974
Roberts, Tom	2001
Robinson, Don	1951
Romeo, Joe	1988
Romeo, Pat	1991
Rosky, Joe	1987
Ruckenbrod, Carl	1927
Rud, Paul	1927
Rudolph, Charles	1965
Ruhlman, Norman	1942
Sanko, Mike	1966
Schneider, Dick	1963
Schuck, Nicholas	2005
Scott, George	
Scot, Murray	1992
Sebest, Bob	
Sedlacko, Vic	1960
Semko, John	1943
Sepsey, Alex	2021
Serich, Shaun	2012
Shaffer, Bill	1965
Shanks, Ed	1988
Shepard, Bob	1958
Sheperd, Ron	
Sherman, Roger	
Shevel, Glen	1956
Shovlin, Frank	1987
Siegfried, Kurt	1990
Silver, Bob	
Simkins, Tyler	2016
Simkins, Bud	1975
Simon, Gil	1939
Skinner, Bill	1958
Slagle, George	1925
Slagle, Orville	1929
Slifka, Larry	1968
Smith, Don	1937
Smith, Harry	1926
Smith, Howard	1926
Smith, R D	1948
Smith, Ralph	1923
Smith, Tommy	1936
Sprinkle, Russel	1933
Stafford, John	1988
Stansbury, Fred	1923
Starn, Don	1943
Steiner, Tony	2002
Stewart, Ralph	1946
Stilson, Steve	2016
Szmara, Ben	1998
Taylor, Charles	1944
Teaberry, Larry	
Terlecki, Tod	2002
Thorp, Jerry	1956
Tierney, Wilbur	1956
Tims, Myron	1941
Titus, Grant	1926
Titus, Ray	1988
Tomalka, Charlie	1959
Tomalka, Jack	1955
Tregurtha, Graham	1965
Trier, J.	1948
Vaughn, George	
Vaughn, Marty	
Walsh, Mike	1990
Weddell, Chester	1938
Wedekind, Charles	1952
Weimer, George	1953
Wharry, Joel	2014
Wheeler, Mark	1987
White, Lynn	1965
Williams, Wayne	1956
Wilson, Jim	1973
Wilson, Jim (Volunteer)	
Wolfe, Jarod	2022
Wolfe, Harry	1997
Wolfecale, Grant	1953
Woolweaver, Kevin	1992
Wright, Bob	1965
Wright, Kurt	1992
Wright, Scott	1990
Wynn, D.	1955
Yanulaitis, Anthony	2015
Yocum, James	2000
Yocum, Jeff	1998
Yoder, William	1965
Zima, Al	1930
Zelanokovic, John	1949
Zimmerman, Carl	1927

✠ *All In The Family* ✠

We have all seen that service in the police and fire departments has become a tradition in many families. So, it should come as no surprise that Boardman Fire Department has plenty of evidence that serving on the fire department is a family affair. I have worked the full spreadsheet of members' names and am happy to share with you the family ties in Boardman Fire Department.

Three families share the distinction of having the most family members who have been firefighters with Boardman Fire Department. The Heintzelman family, the Nordquist family, and the Smith family had five members on the department.

The Heintzelman family- H. C. (Henry Clinton) Heintzelman was one of the founders of our department. This highly esteemed member of Boardman Township suffered the loss of his entire home in 1921 to a raging fire. No doubt this was his and his family's motivation in urging Boardman to form a fire department. It should be no surprise that H.C. and his sons Ken and Fay plus his nephew Howard Kyle all were listed among our founding fathers. Later, H. C.'s son John joined the fire department making **five members** of the Heintzelman family Boardman firefighters. Smith Dairy had always been supportive of the fire department. One of the projects included the Dairy joining in partnership with the firefighters to purchase gas masks for the department.

The Nordquist family- Sig (Siegfried) Nordquist was voted by the club members in 1926 to be permitted to join the department. He became a valued member of the department. Up until 1955, the department fire officers were voted into position annually by the club membership. Sig Nordquist was elected to the position of Assistant Chief every time he ran. Along with Sig joining the department in 1926 were his twin brothers Clarence and Lawrence. Lawrence, who also held the nickname of Swede, is the father of Dale Nordquist. Larry became the second person in the department to achieve full-time status when he was appointed on January 5, 1944, to serve as Merle Gifford's Assistant Chief. In 1989, Dale Nordquist, his son, joined the department as a volunteer firefighter. Also, a member of the Nordquist family was Robert Pugh whose nickname in 1956, was Butch. Butch was a half-brother of Dale. Butch worked across the street from the main fire station and was in a good location to get to the fire station quickly when a fire came in. This adds up to **five family members**.

The Smith family- The Smith family was important to Boardman Fire Department. Not only were five of the family members firefighters, but the Smith Dairy retail shop was less than 100' from the fire station. The Smiths must have felt a special kinship with the department because they were quick to volunteer to help with a project or offer funding when the fire department was short of funds. Before the first fire station was ever built, the Smiths permitted the fire department to store the two-wheeled fire wagon in a garage behind the Dairy's shop. Smith Dairy donated an old milk truck to the Junior firefighters for their use. Harry Smith 1926 father of Howard Smith 1926, Tommy Smith 1936, Caroll Smith, 1950, and Don Smith 1957.

The following family had four members in the department.

- Red Neapolitan 1937, Bob Neapolitan 1949, Billy Neapolitan 1953, and Donny Neapolitan 1953.

The following families had three members in the department.

- Kermit Carlson 1925, Quinton Carlson 1926, and Chester Carlson 1929.
- Myron Davis 1926 and brother Bales Davis 1927, Bob Davis 1961 whose father was Myron. Myron lived on Washington Boulevard at the same time as the Southern Park Racetrack was booming. He served as an electrician for the grounds.
- Jack deSaulles 1938, son Assistant Chief J.B. deSaulles 1955, and Kathy May/Kachmer 1992 stepdaughter to J.B. deSaulles.
- Bob Ewing 1951, Harold Ewing 1952, and Chief Wayne Ewing 1954.
- Albert Hanna 1937, Bill Hanna 1950, and Dave Hanna 1950.
- Frank Powell 1928, Paul Powell 1937, P. Powell 1948.
- Bob Wright 1963 father of Scott Wright 1990 and Kurt Wright 1996.

The following families had two members with the department.

- Bert Alexander 1926 and Melvin Alexander 1927, brothers Francis Buckley 1965 and Chuck Buckley 1968, brothers Ed Bush 1949 and Assistant Chief Bill Bush 1954, Paul Cartright 1940 and Ed Cartright 1941, Chief Don Cover 1943 and his son Dave Cover 1966, Dick Dorman 1966 father of Chief Jim Dorman 1968, Frank Dustman 1926 and Paul Dustman 1927, Blaine Heaven 1956 and Ron Heaven 1956, Fred Hoover 1965 and his son Jim Hoover 1995, Captain Bill Manley Sr. 1957 and his son Bill Manley Jr. 1980, Frank Mesmer 1937 and Vern Mesmer 1961, Harry Morgan 1943 and Gary Morgan 1986, Roy Parker 1929 and Bill Parker 1943, Paul Reed 1927 and Frank Reed 1929, Assistant Chief Joe Romeo 1987 and brother Captain Pat Romeo 1991, George Slagle 1925 and Orville Slagle 1929, Jack Tomalka 1955 and Assistant Chief Charlie Tomalka 1959, Harry Wolfe 1997 and son Jarod Wolfe 2022, Earl Zimmerman 1927 and Lou Zimmerman 1927.

✠ *Significant Fires* ✠

A house catches fire and burns to the ground. This is what Boardman residents faced before the fire department was founded. Boardman Fire Department was formed to do something about these disasters. Over the 100 years that our fire department served the community, houses and other structures still burned, sustaining heavy damage and even occasionally burning to the ground. These heavy losses occurred primarily because the fire had a substantial head start before the fire department was notified.

As equipment improved, so did the ability of firefighters to get a fire knocked down quickly and save buildings even though the fire may be large. But even today, in 2023, we will still experience heavy fire losses from time to time. *Significant Fires* shows the reader fires with high dollar losses. But *Significant Fires* also records fires where people lost their lives. The dollar loss may have been low but a fire death always has a significant impact on both family members and the firefighters who fought to save the lives.

- December 11, 1930 — Hitchcock barn, the largest in Ohio, lost 18 prize cows-$20,000
- December 3, 1953 — Stambaugh Thompson, Boardman Plaza- $300,000
- February 9, 1961 — Town Hall, Rectory and Boardman News, 7354 Market-$10,000
- January 1, 1963 — Aerolite Extrusions, 4605 Lake Park Road-$250,000
- April 12, 1965 — Boardman Lumberyard, Southern Boulevard and 224-$75,000
- April 3, 1969 — Scotford Volkswagen, 4845 Market Street-$250,000
- April 4, 1972 — Randal Good bombing 4902 Brookwood Avenue-$70,000
- December 29, 1972 — Plakie Toy, 4105 Simon Road-extensive structural damage
- January 31, 1973 — Batos building, 75 Karago-arson, multiple gas cans-$30,000
- February 20, 1973 — Joseph Bucheit Company, 4040 Simon Road- explosion-$150,000+
- February 1, 1974 — Residence under construction, 795 Squirrel Hill-total loss-$30,500
- February 28, 1974 — Arena Bowling Lanes, 3980 Simon Road- heavy fog- $500,000
- September 29, 1974 — Hillman Way Center, 4011 Hillman Way- $23,000
- March 21, 1975 — Batos building-floor drops 12" firefighters inside- $100,000
- Summer 1977 — 6-Plex apartments under construction, Bonnie Place-$48,000
- February 15, 1979 — Master's fire, 32 Sciota- murdered wife and house a total loss
- September 12, 1980 — Gasoline tank explosion, 439 Oak Avenue- two injured-$80,000
- November 17, 1983 — Mansion, 73 Newport Drive-heavy damage-$100,000
- May 20, 1985 — Beaver Township Illegal fireworks site- explosion, six dead
- December 24, 1986 — Rossi Furniture, 6000 block South Avenue-$500,000
- March 1, 1987 — Edgar Miller Company, 1236 Velma Court-$445,000
- September 19, 1987 — Stambaugh Thompson Lighting- largest loss-$2,500,000
- November 2, 1989 — Marwood Office Center, 6215- 6255 Markets Street-$550,000
- March 11, 1990 — Diamond Steel, 8270 Raub Avenue- gas explosion-$250,000
- February 7, 1997 — Carpet Remnant Room, Simon Road-Arson-$2,000,000
- October 9, 1997 — Jade Court Restaurant, 1984 Boardman-Poland Road-$200,000

- January 17, 1998 Maag Mansion, Boardman Poland Road- historical home- $3,000
- August 24, 2002 Saint James Church-steeple Boardman Park lightning-$250,000
- August 8, 2003 Industrial fire to lathe, 690 McClurg Road-$150,000
- March 2, 2006 UPS Store, 143 Boardman Canfield Road-Arson-$200,000
- November 7, 2006 Residence, 4370 Yakata Dora-Arson-$202,000
- November 14, 2006 Residence, 142 Mathews Road-$150,000
- June 11, 2007 Manufacturing Building, 8469 Southern Boulevard-$500,000
- July 9, 2007 Residence, 1460 Tori Pines Court-$500,000
- June 20, 2008 Residence, 4370 Yakata Dora- second fire in two years- 500,000
- June 26, 2009 Battery Powered Dragster, 8431 South Avenue-$150,000
- January 8, 2010 Residence, 820 Southwestern Run-$353,000
- March 12, 2011 Residence, 6592 Mill Creek Boulevard-Basement-$175,000
- April 26, 2011 Residence, 75 Prestwick Drive-$165,000
- March 18, 2012 D&D Industrial, 225 McClurg Road-fireman shocked-$950,000
- January 28, 2013 Mill Creek Village, 6849 Lockwood Boulevard-one death- $900,000
- October 8, 2013 Spice of India, 8398 Market Street- Arson four convicted/jailed-$225,000
- June 17, 2014 Allstate/Subway building, 8162 Market Street-$1,100,000
- December 16, 2015 Residence, 5731 Border Avenue-suicide death-$3,000
- April 19, 2016 Newport Glen, 4071 Glenwood Avenue- one death-$75,000
- February 12, 2017 Condo, 1100 Boardman Canfield Road-suicide attempt-$250,000
- March 9, 2017 Residence, 8260 Southern Boulevard-unattended candle-$160,000
- April 24 2018 Tiffany's Bar and Grill, 7080 Tiffany Boulevard-$505,000
- March 15, 2019 Donnell Ford, 7955 Market Street-$1,000,000
- March 15, 2019 Townhouses, 337 Mathews Road-two rescued-$110,000
- May 20, 2019 Townhouses, 335 Mathews Road-Suspicious fire-$180,000
- August 12, 2019 Boardman Towing, 702 McClurg Road-$450,000
- April 24, 2022 Apartments, 4111 Glenwood Avenue-four rescued-$150,000
- February 3, 2023 East Palestine, Ohio- major train derailment and fire-millions lost

✠ *Fire Deaths* ✠

The goals of all fire departments are to save lives, property and protect the environment. We do our best to accomplish all three but at times we are not always successful. The number one goal is to save lives but sometimes circumstances prevent us from achieving this objective. We have saved so many more lives than have been lost in fires. We feel anger and sadness every time someone dies.

The following is an accounting of the fire deaths that have been recorded in Boardman Fire Department's history.

1927 The first fire death on record occurred in 1927 when George Best and his brother were sent to the barn, on Simon Road, to throw hay from the loft for the cows. One of the boys had been playing with matches. The hay caught on fire and George hid in a toolbox. He died in the wooden box. His brother was burned but survived.

1945 A run report indicates a woman died from her burns she sustained when a trash burner she was tending caused a field fire.

1961 The Annual Report indicated an unidentified fire death.

1962 Former firefighter, Dave Amon described this incident. There was a home fully involved in fire. He and Barney Davison entered the house and searched for a female victim. They found her and pulled her out but she suffered burns all over most of her body from which she died.

1964 The annual report for 1964 mentions that there was one death due to fire this year. No other details have been found.

1968 At midnight, 85 year old Edith Saarbach died in a fire in her home. The recluse was a hoarder. She had saved stacks of newspapers, magazines, clothes, cans of food, and stacks of her writing. This made good fuel for the fire. When firefighters arrived, flames were coming out of the downstairs windows. The fire was put out in 15 minutes. Firemen donned air packs and searched for the victim. She was found in her kitchen which was undamaged. Mrs. Saarbach died of smoke inhalation. The fire damage was only $5,000.

1972 Randal Good was associated with the criminal elements in the area. The 24 year old was on a 5

year probation for transporting stolen goods. But he was also a confidential informant. His snitching was known by the mobsters and they either set out to

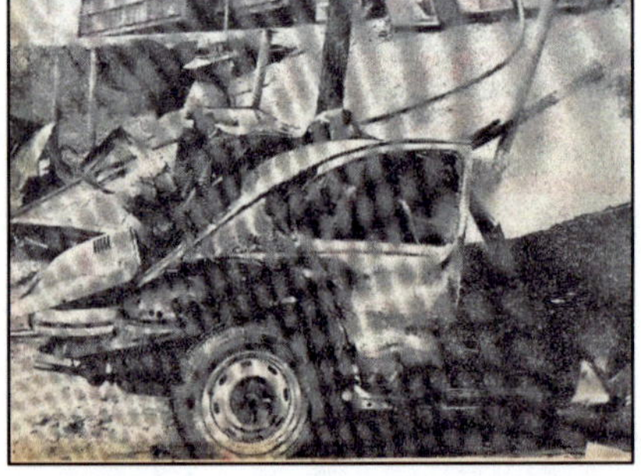

kill him or send him a message. An unexploded bomb was found under the hood of his car at a service station.

Apparently, he didn't get the message. Days later, on April 5th Good, his wife, and his friend got into his Volkswagen Beetle. When he started the car, the bomb under his seat went off and killed him instantly. The explosion blew the gasoline from his car all over the Brookwood Road apartment building where his car was parked. The other two occupants were injured in the explosion and fire but they survived. The fire was fought for hours. The ATF was called in because it was a bombing. The damage to the apartment building was estimated to be $70,000. Even though Good sustained burns to 99% of his body, his cause of death was the bomb under his seat.

1975 Mrs. Bertha Prine was a smoker. While she was working in the kitchen of her house on Walker Mill Road around noon on September 2nd, she must have dropped her cigarette on her nylon blouse which caught fire. The fire spread to the rest of her clothing. Her daughter found her on the kitchen floor and her clothing had all burned away. The fire victim had died of smoke asphyxiation even though she had sustained second and third-degree burns over 75% of her body. No fire damage occurred to the kitchen.

1975 Mrs. Edna Winter lived on Shields Road. The only record that could be found of her death was in her obituary of December 2nd. She died in her home during a kitchen fire. Nothing else is known about the circumstances related to her death or the fire.

1979 Stephen Masters, who lived on Sciota Avenue, was convicted of the murder of his wife Jodi on Valentine's Day. The two nineteen year old kids had been recently married. Stephen was convicted of shooting his wife in her bed with a rifle. He doused her body and the bedroom with gasoline and left a gasoline trail to the front door. He then set the house on fire. The fire was put out, but not before several firefighters sustained injuries in a backdraft which knocked them down a set of steps. Masters had taken out a $100,000 insurance policy on his wife three days before the murder. After a lengthy trial, where numerous firefighters gave testimony, Masters was convicted and sentenced to 25 years in prison. Even though Mrs. Masters sustained major burns over 100% of her body, the cause of death was bullet wounds.

1987 On March 9th, the family of Henry Pilewicz had gotten together at his Meadowbrook Avenue home. He smelled smoke and found that the back section of his basement was on fire. He led his family consisting of his wife, daughter, son-in-law, and two very young grandchildren out of the house. They all were treated for smoke inhalation. Pilewicz called the fire department from a neighbor's house and then went back into the basement to fight the fire. The smoke overcame him and he died on the basement floor of smoke inhalation. Firefighters worked hard to get him up out of the basement but to no avail. The fire loss was only $5,000 but the electrical fire produced heavy toxic smoke. This is why firefighters say once out of a burning home, stay out!

2013 Shawna Carney lived at the Mill Creek Village Apartments on Lockwood Boulevard. Around 8:00 in the morning, residents were alerted by the hallway smoke detectors. Most seemed unaware of the fire until firefighters knocked on their doors and ordered them to leave. When the fire department arrived, flames were shooting from the roof of the apartment complex. Carney was rescued from her apartment and taken to the hospital where she later died from smoke inhalation. There was a portable oxygen tank and a liquid oxygen refill bottle in the room but it is unknown if the O2 was a contributing factor in the spread of the fire.

2015 On December 16th Andrew Gallagher who was 37, was found chained by his ankle to his toilet on the second floor bathroom. His Border Avenue home was on fire. Chief Pitzer said of the 4:00 a.m. fire, "The first arriving companies saw heavy fire involvement throughout the structure. Gallagher had to be identified by his dental records. The coroner believed that he initially died of smoke inhalation and carbon monoxide poisoning. He had tried to commit suicide in the past. The fire had extended to all rooms of the home. It had to be demolished."

2016 Firefighters were called to the Newport Glen apartment of Curtis Cochrane and his wife on Glenwood Avenue. Reports were that there was smoke in the halls. More than 60 people were evacuated from the complex. Youngstown, Poland, Canfield, and Beaver fire departments assisted in the fire control. The couple was pulled from their second floor apartment. Mr. Cochrane later died and his wife was in critical condition from smoke inhalation. The fire had started in the kitchen and spread to the dining room.

Twelve people have died in Boardman due to fire. Additionally, two more people were murdered and their remains were consumed in fire. The cause of these fires is a mix and bad acts and poor decisions.

Excerpts From 1953 Training Manual

Training is a big part of what all firefighters do regularly to remain proficient in day to day firefighting skills. Just like an athlete or an astronaut, training prepares us for our jobs and assures that every member of the team, no matter what type of team it is, performs his or her job to the best of their ability.

In 1939, the State of Ohio developed a training manual simply titled Fire Service Training. In our department, almost every minute of our training was based on the skills and techniques presented in this book. Our firefighters knew the book inside and out. The following are a few of the pages from a 1953 manual to show the reader what we learned and a glimpse at the manual.

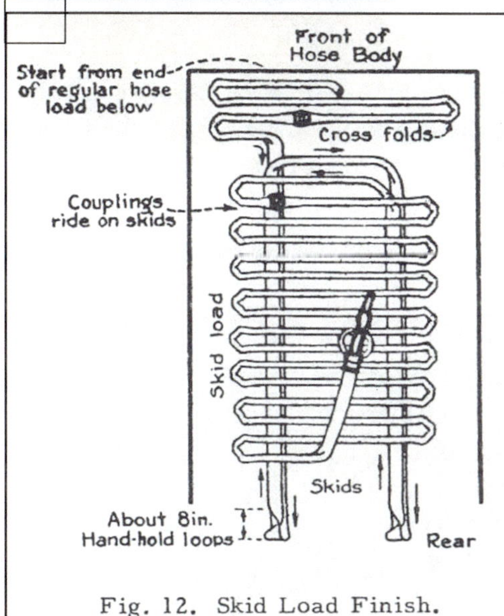

Fig. 12. Skid Load Finish.

Skid loads provide a pre-connected fire attack line which combines a larger hose, for water supply with smaller hoses for flexibility. It pulls off the truck in one load and can be deployed in less than a minute.

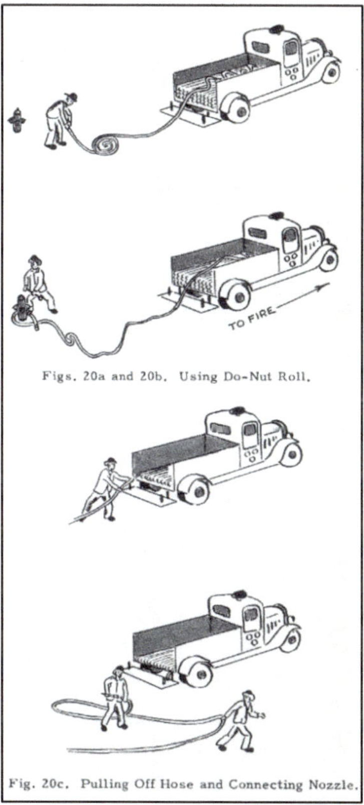

Figs. 20a and 20b. Using Do-Nut Roll.

Fig. 20c. Pulling Off Hose and Connecting Nozzle.

Pictorial showing how to use a Do-Nut hose roll to connect the truck to a hydrant.

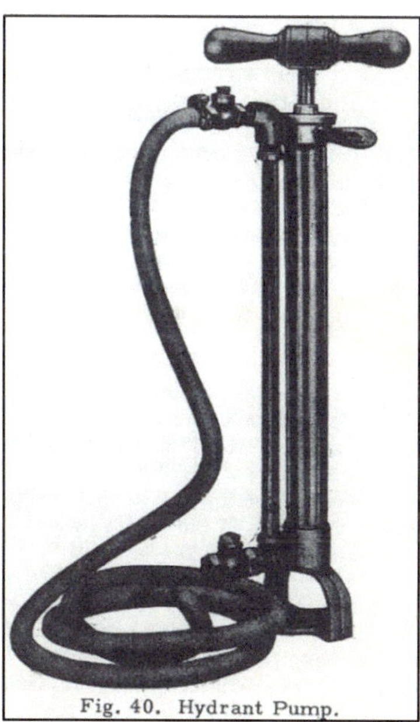

Fig. 40. Hydrant Pump.

A hydrant pump is used to pump the barrel of a hydrant out in the winter after it has been used. This helps keep the hydrant from freezing. We used a hydrant pump many times in the winter.

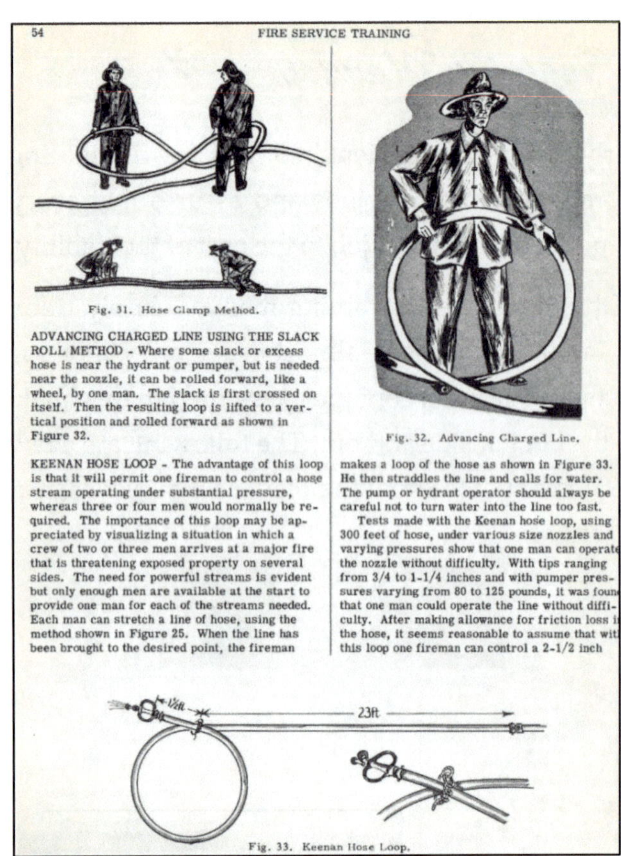

54 FIRE SERVICE TRAINING

Fig. 31. Hose Clamp Method.

ADVANCING CHARGED LINE USING THE SLACK ROLL METHOD - Where some slack or excess hose is near the hydrant or pumper, but is needed near the nozzle, it can be rolled forward, like a wheel, by one man. The slack is first crossed on itself. Then the resulting loop is lifted to a vertical position and rolled forward as shown in Figure 32.

Fig. 32. Advancing Charged Line.

KEENAN HOSE LOOP - The advantage of this loop is that it will permit one fireman to control a hose stream operating under substantial pressure, whereas three or four men would normally be required. The importance of this loop may be appreciated by visualizing a situation in which a crew of two or three men arrives at a major fire that is threatening exposed property on several sides. The need for powerful streams is evident but only enough men are available at the start to provide one man for each of the streams needed. Each man can stretch a line of hose, using the method shown in Figure 25. When the line has been brought to the desired point, the fireman makes a loop of the hose as shown in Figure 33. He then straddles the line and calls for water. The pump or hydrant operator should always be careful not to turn water into the line too fast.

Tests made with the Keenan hose loop, using 300 feet of hose, under various size nozzles and varying pressures show that one man can operate the nozzle without difficulty. With tips ranging from 3/4 to 1-1/4 inches and with pumper pressures varying from 80 to 125 pounds, it was found that one man could operate the line without difficulty. After making allowance for friction loss in the hose, it seems reasonable to assume that with this loop one fireman can control a 2-1/2 inch

Fig. 33. Keenan Hose Loop.

This shows how to advance hose that is full of water. A Keenan Hose Loop is a method that allows one firefighter to sit on and control a large diameter hose line that normally takes three people.

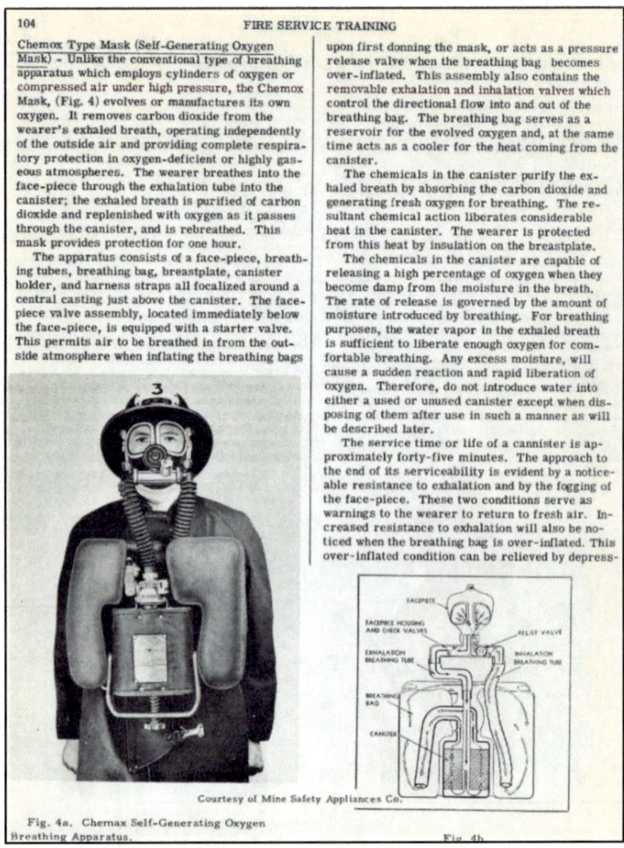

104 FIRE SERVICE TRAINING

Chemox Type Mask (Self-Generating Oxygen Mask) - Unlike the conventional type of breathing apparatus which employs cylinders of oxygen or compressed air under high pressure, the Chemox Mask, (Fig. 4) evolves or manufactures its own oxygen. It removes carbon dioxide from the wearer's exhaled breath, operating independently of the outside air and providing complete respiratory protection in oxygen-deficient or highly gaseous atmospheres. The wearer breathes into the face-piece through the exhalation tube into the canister; the exhaled breath is purified of carbon dioxide and replenished with oxygen as it passes through the canister, and is rebreathed. This mask provides protection for one hour.

The apparatus consists of a face-piece, breathing tubes, breathing bag, breastplate, canister holder, and harness straps all focalized around a central casting just above the canister. The face-piece valve assembly, located immediately below the face-piece, is equipped with a starter valve. This permits air to be breathed in from the outside atmosphere when inflating the breathing bags upon first donning the mask, or acts as a pressure release valve when the breathing bag becomes over-inflated. This assembly also contains the removable exhalation and inhalation valves which control the directional flow into and out of the breathing bag. The breathing bag serves as a reservoir for the evolved oxygen and, at the same time acts as a cooler for the heat coming from the canister.

The chemicals in the canister purify the exhaled breath by absorbing the carbon dioxide and generating fresh oxygen for breathing. The resultant chemical action liberates considerable heat in the canister. The wearer is protected from this heat by insulation on the breastplate.

The chemicals in the canister are capable of releasing a high percentage of oxygen when they become damp from the moisture in the breath. The rate of release is governed by the amount of moisture introduced by breathing. For breathing purposes, the water vapor in the exhaled breath is sufficient to liberate enough oxygen for comfortable breathing. Any excess moisture, will cause a sudden reaction and rapid liberation of oxygen. Therefore, do not introduce water into either a used or unused canister except when disposing of them after use in such a manner as will be described later.

The service time or life of a cannister is approximately forty-five minutes. The approach to the end of its serviceability is evident by a noticeable resistance to exhalation and by the fogging of the face-piece. These two conditions serve as warnings to the wearer to return to fresh air. Increased resistance to exhalation will also be noticed when the breathing bag is over-inflated. This over-inflated condition can be relieved by depress-

Courtesy of Mine Safety Appliances Co.

Fig. 4a. Chemax Self-Generating Oxygen Breathing Apparatus.

Fig. 4b

Instructions on how to use a Chemox type of air pack. In 1968, when I first got on, there was one Chemox still in the department, but it was no longer in use.

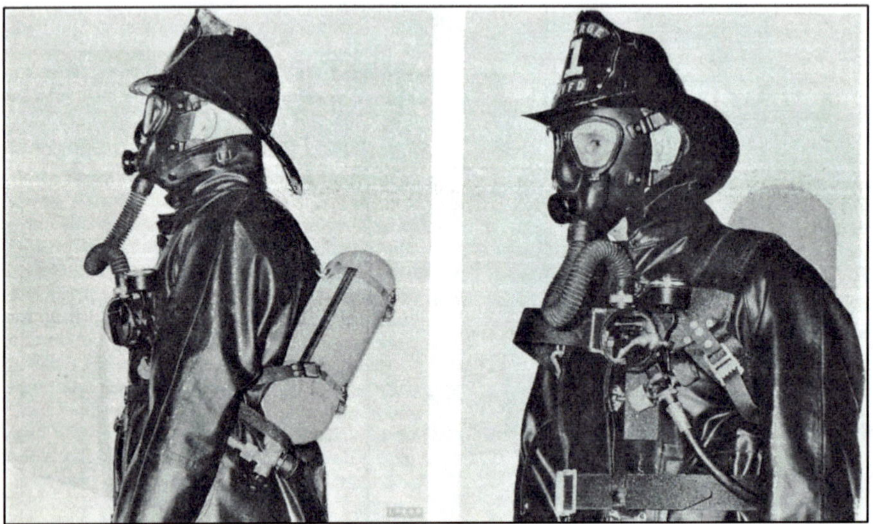

Pictured is a sling pack named for the way which it is put on. It only had about 15 minutes of air in the bottle. Officers used it to take a quick look inside a building on fire to determine their course of action. All fire departments removed them from trucks after the NFPA recommended their removal because of their limited air supply.

I was taught from the 1968 version of the fire service training manual. We spent a lot of time in what we called "The Black Book". Most of the lessons in my book were the same as in the 1953 version.

In a 1957 "Letter to the Editor" Chief Gifford wrote, "As for training, our paid men as well as our 30 volunteer firemen, have received training by the Ohio State Vocational Education Training Program. Drills are held every week with the men receiving training on all phases of firefighting. A complete library is available to the men with the latest newsletters, bulletins, folders, and fire codes being received from state and national fire protection organizations daily." This has been a tradition followed by Boardman Fire Chiefs to this day.

In 1978, the IFSTA training manual (International Fire Service Training Academy) became the primary source of training materials for the fire service. The IFSTA Essentials of Firefighting replaced our Fire Service Training manual. Each major chapter is printed as its own book. In all, there are 29 IFSTA manuals available to choose from.

✠ Founding Dates of Mahoning County Fire Departments ✠

Every fire department loves to learn about its history and nothing is more important than the department's founding date. Here are the 21 fire departments in Mahoning County and the date each was formed.

1868 Youngstown

1900 Struthers

1901 Sebring

1906 Lowellville

1923 Boardman

1923 Poland and the Western Reserve Joint Fire District formed in 1984.

1926 Campbell originally was called East Youngstown. The East Youngstown Fire Department was reorganized under the new city name, Campbell in 1959.

1927 Beaver

1932 Canfield and the Cardinal Joint Fire District were formed in 1998.

1938 Austintown

1946 New Middletown, Springfield, and Petersburg collaborated to purchase three pumper trucks, one for each community. This became the first organized fire department for each. In 1972, the communities dissolved the common relationship, and Springfield and New Middletown formed their own department. Unincorporated Petersburg is taken care of by Springfield.

1943 Green

1947 Berlin

1948 Craig Beach

1951 Ellsworth

1952 Beloit

1953 Jackson

1956 Damascus

1958 Coitsville

2000 Milton

Excerpts from "That's The Way It Was" 

Boardman's Early Citizens Share Stories About Boardman And The Fire Department-

In 1976, Dick Lalumia and John Moore published a book titled, "That's The Way It Was, Historical Highlights of Boardman Township." In the process, at least 72 prominent Boardman citizens were interviewed and recorded onto cassette tapes. Many of those people spoke of their time in Boardman in the 1920s and 1930s. Here are some of the excerpts from those interviews which include comments about matters related to Boardman Fire Department as well as a glimpse into life in the early 1900s"s.

The first Fire Chief, Merle Gifford, and his wife Lucy both contribute.–

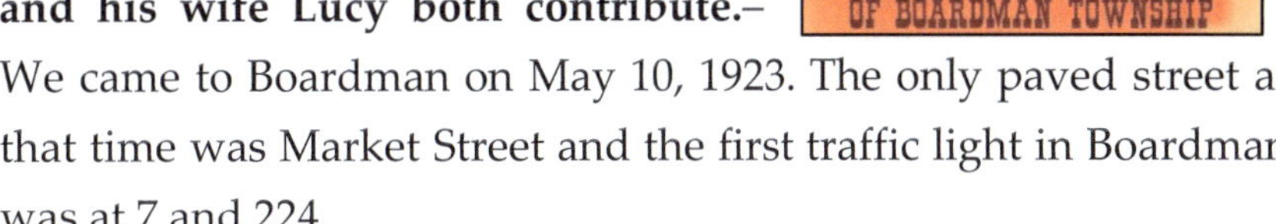

We came to Boardman on May 10, 1923. The only paved street at that time was Market Street and the first traffic light in Boardman was at 7 and 224.

We attended the Methodist Church for a long time. This was located just south of 224 on the west side of the street. We later switched to Calvary Baptist located on Ridge and Oak Hill Avenue. The services were a little bit longer than they are today and we had quite a few members. But there were not that many houses, from 224 to Midlothian. You could probably count all the houses on two hands. There was also the Episcopal Church, that one that is down there in the park, it was across the street. Many people went there. There was one room for the congregation and one room for Sunday school. The parents sat with their kids for Sunday school because it was first. Services lasted about an hour. There was a choir made up of men and women.

We remember the snowstorm of 1950. There was 34 – 36" of snow. We also had a lot of basement flooding during large storms. We (the fire department) were always out all night pumping them.

We almost were the first grocery store but Catherman's across from the school and Zimmer Brothers were the first. My store was located near Southern Boulevard on 224 right next door to the fire station. We sold meats and gasoline. (Gifford's gas station is described as the first service station in the Township.) We had a butcher (Carl Apple) and another man who helped us. We delivered. They called up and we took it to them. If you forgot something you would have to make another trip. We had a little Dodge truck. Mrs. Gifford didn't make the deliveries, I did. We were open 7 days a week from 6:30 a.m. to about 10:00 p.m. or a little later. The cost of a loaf of bread was a nickel and milk was ten cents a quart and it came in a glass bottle.

In 1923, Market Street was from the center south, just a brick road on one side. I am very familiar with the Southern Park Racetrack. It was a very active spot back in the mid to late twenties. The Y & S streetcar ran out there, crowded, for the afternoon races. The races were all in the daytime back then. A serious fire occurred in 1924 that burned three barns and destroyed 9 horses. We used to go to the Bannowbrook dancehall. For entertainment at home, we used to get around a piano and sing, had card parties, took bridge lessons, and played 500 and canasta.

On Boardman Fire Department: The fire department originated on September 10, 1923, in front of Boardman Supply office where it is now. We had a two-wheel cart which they pulled behind a coal truck. It had two forty gallon tanks mounted on it and later they were mounted on a Ford Model T. When asked how much water the trucks held he replied 500 gallons but the town only wanted to have 50 gallons on the truck. The fire trucks had Boardman Fire Department lettering on the side. I served as Fire Chief from September 10, 1923, to January 1, 1961, almost 38 years.

The third **Fire Chief, Don Cover** – Then they decided they needed some fire equipment. They first set up on the corner of Southern Boulevard and Route 224. There was a little grocery store there that Gifford ran at the time. They had a shed by the grocery store and that's where they put their first piece of equipment. This was back in 1923.

The first piece of equipment was like a trailer. The men would grab hold and pull it along. On this trailer was a large tank which was like a soda and acid fire extinguisher. That's where they got the pressure. They didn't have pumps on the truck so the soda and acid extinguisher gave them the pressure. They'd grab that trailer and run after the fire. If they weren't too tired when they got there, they'd try to put the fire out if the building wasn't already burned down.

Back in the time, they didn't have any money for a paid department so, of course, it was all volunteer. Even the Chief was a volunteer. Mr. Merle Gifford became the first Fire Chief. They scrounged around to get what they could for the fire department. The men just got together. There was no pay for anybody. They were lucky if they had gasoline for their fire equipment at that time.

The firemen lived at home and the fire department bought a siren that they set on top of a pole by the fire station. Of course, they had someone to receive the fire calls and they in turn would blow the whistle. That would tell all the firemen that they had a fire and they would run to the station. (Whistle was a slang term the firemen used for the siren.)

I was never a Junior fireman. I worked with the Junior firemen. That was organized after I became a full-time volunteer. The Junior firemen pretty much learned about firefighting. They learned some of the techniques of firefighting. They learned about the equipment and the fire gear. They could do everything except go into a burning building. They knew how to roll hose and how to take care of it. And, of course, they knew how to polish the trucks too.

This fire station, where we are conducting the interview, was the first real fire station. It was the one that was built about 1927. This was a small part of the present station, right in the center here. It was built partly with Township funds and partly with funds the men raised themselves with fish fries and things of that nature that they used to have.

Our fire equipment has changed. I mentioned the old soda and acid fire truck. We've progressed into the first motorized fire equipment. And that was a Model T Ford. The Model T Ford also had a soda and acid fire extinguisher on it. Finally, in 1927, the Township bought the first real fire truck. This was a Seagrave fire truck. It didn't have a windshield on it and it didn't have a cab on it. The men sat right out in the open. It did have a pump, a 500 gallon a minute pump. It also had a water tank, so they had some water they took with them. With the pump, you could develop the pressure as necessary and they could do a pretty good job of fighting fires. This type of truck progressed into the very modern trucks such as we have now. We have a heavy squad truck for rescue and salvage. We have the heavy pumper. One pumper we have will pump 2000 gallons of water a minute. It's diesel powered. We have another truck they used to call a hook and ladder, but now we have an elevated platform fire truck. This puts the men over a building where they can get to the fire or can reach fire on a high rise building.

In the fire department's history, I am the third Fire Chief. Since Merle Gifford, we had Wayne Ewing who was the Fire Chief from 1960-1965. I have been the only one since then. So, there have been only three of us. We had a very nice dinner, the fiftieth anniversary of the fire department, and all three Fire Chiefs were present at that dinner.

A Fire Chief is hopefully appointed based on his knowledge of the fire service. When the job opens up, the Trustees of the Township pick out who they feel they want to do the job of running the fire department. They look for a combination of firefighting knowledge and administrative experience.

The first time a firefighter was appointed as a paid man occurred back in 1955. I think that they started putting on full-time men. They had the firemen act as dispatchers too. So, the first firemen were working on the desk at the fire station on Market Street and they were doing the dispatching for the fire department. In other words, if you had a fire, you'd call up and those men would answer the phone. Of course, if there was a fire, they would get somebody else to cover the phone while they were out fighting the fire. They were a little bit shorthanded back in those days.

They built the first real fire station in 1927. They moved out of the little shed that they had and moved into the new fire station. In 1937, they built a station on Market Street which is the present police station. Sometime later, because of Mill Creek and the inability to get a truck over into the Cornersburg area, they built a fire station on Shields Road and Lockwood Boulevard. Because of the railroad track and the industrial area, on Lake Park Road, they built a station on South Avenue and Mathews Road, which became the fourth station. Later we saw the development of the south end of the Township which we didn't have before. We saw the need for some improved coverage there and since our three stations on the north end were grouped together, we eliminated the fire equipment in the station on Market Street and built up the station near the center of the Township on Route 224 across from the Mall. We concentrated our equipment and manpower at this central station so we could better cover the south end of the Township.

The motivation for organizing the fire department was that Boardman had suffered a couple of very bad fires. Firefighting is an expensive operation. But at the loss of a couple of homes, the people realized that they had to do something. They had to keep their homes from burning to the ground. There was a case of a fire in a house on the corner of 224 and Southern Boulevard. They called the Youngstown Fire Department. Of course, with the lack of speed of the equipment back in those days and the conditions of the roads, by the time the truck got out here from Youngstown, the house was a total loss. So, some of the public-spirited men in the community decide they'd have to do something for themselves. They got together and organized a department so they'd have some kind of fire protection and hoped that they could get to fires before they could get too bad to put them out. I think this is part of the United States, people waiting too long for someone else to do something for them. So, then they just decided to do it for themselves. The department became one of the leaders in the area as a volunteer fire department as far as advanced technique and firefighting knowledge that they had and all without pay.

There have been a lot of changes in the equipment that we have used over the years. I mentioned that several years ago, we had the chemical or soda and acid truck. You know they've never found anything better than water for putting out fires, not as far as an all-around firefighting agent. Many, many years ago they had the town pump, the watering trough out by the town pump. When they had a fire, all the residents of the town would get together and form a bucket brigade. One fellow would get a bucket of water out of the trough and pass it to the next man and they'd keep passing it. The man near the fire would throw the bucket of water at the fire. It usually didn't put it out. The bucket was too small. We carry water with us. We get water from our fire hydrants, which is another big advancement in firefighting equipment. The fire hydrants you see along the street are our provide of water. It's the same water you drink in the house and use for cooking. So there really hasn't been much change in the material we use to fight the big fires. For small fires, we now have dry powder fire extinguishers and we have CO2 extinguishers. These items are for specialized use depending on what the fire is and they're for very small fires.

Our fire hydrants were put in many years ago but I don't specifically know when. They used to call them fire plugs years ago. There was a plug that was down in a holding area like a cistern and they'd pull the plug and drop the hose down in and pump the water out of this tank and this is how they originally got the name fireplug. Now we call them fire hydrants because they're hooked to a network of pipes. The pipes can go anywhere from four inches in diameter to possibly three feet in diameter.

This is for distributing large quantities of water. We have a bigger size hose on the truck, three or four inches or larger hoses to connect onto the hydrants with. They used to be all two and a half inch hoses. Speaking of hoses, many years ago the only material they had to make a hose out of was leather. You can imagine trying to make a suitable hose and take care of it when it's made out of leather material. They'd staple or rivet it together and of course, they couldn't have very long lengths of it. The making of a hose was a slow process. I suppose there was somebody, maybe a harness maker, who would put together a leather hose. I've seen pictures of them and I've seen them on display, but I've never had to use them. They did the best they could and they've advanced tremendously. I can remember as a kid going to watch some of the fires that the firemen got called out on. I can remember a farm down on McClurg Road. It's the same farm the Kessler Products has their factory on. I can remember the very large barn fire on the Hitchcock Farm. It was one of the well-known farms in Boardman Township. It was one of the early homes in Boardman. It was the home of one of the early settlers, I believe Mr. Boardman owned the house and farm before the Hitchcocks. There was a very large barn fire there where they lost a lot of cattle in the fire. Through the years, we always remember the spectacular barn fires. There was one on the Merribell Farm that many old-timers remember. It was on South Avenue. More recently we've had fires such as the Arena.

We had a fire in the Plaza on 224. Of course, there have been tragedies in the loss of homes and the loss of lives. Many times, people lost their lives trying to fight fires or because they couldn't get out. Thank goodness, in Boardman, we haven't had too many fire deaths. There have been two of them in the last ten years. I can remember only three deaths prior to my term as Fire Chief.

Our response to fires has gotten better over the years. To get there on time, we have to be called on time. Our whole operation depends on people calling us to get out there on time. We have a response time of anywhere from one to five minutes. On the far corners of the Township, such as Tippecanoe

Road and Western Reserve Road, it can take us up to seven minutes to get there. Contrary to what most people believe, we're lucky if we can go up to 30 M.P.H. by the time we have to slow down for corners and traffic. We strive to get there before the damage is too bad. The whole fire service is set up to get there as quickly as possible based on the time when we are called.

The types of calls we go on now are much different from those we had to respond to years ago. Many years ago, one of the most serious fire problems we had was the woods or grass fires. With the many acres of open ground, there was the possibility of the fire spreading back to the woods with no way to get the trucks back there. We might spend hours or sometimes days fighting a fire in this situation. One of the greatest stands of timber in the State of Ohio was in Boardman from the Boardman Park extending to the entire southern section of Boardman. In 1897, a fire occurred in these woods, and the entire Boardman area was covered in a dense cloud of smoke for days. This was considered a calamity because one of the finest stands of timber in Ohio had been destroyed. With the buildup of Boardman now, we very seldom have this type of fire. There's also a change in the thinking of people. Now you're not supposed to do any outside burning. Many years ago in the spring, we'd have as many as fifteen grass fires a day. We'd be tied up all day. Thank you I enjoyed the interview.

Elbert Agnew was born in 1915. He became a farmer on the family homestead. Around 1925, we could drive at the age of 14 without a license. The entertainment was listening on a crystal radio to various shows. In the twenties, Market Street (the old Boardman Street named as it was the access road from Youngstown to Boardman) was a two lane road as was Route 224 all other roads were not paved.

In describing the first fire equipment, he said "We had an old Ford with a couple of hundred gallon water tank on it and a lot of volunteer firemen that would put out small fires but it wasn't set up to put out barn fires. In 1920, we had a little section where all the Agnew buildings were burned down except the Agnew house. Nine buildings and two silos were burned down. Our present barn was built in 1920 and at the time, there was no fire department except Canfield. By the time they got here, the buildings were all burned down.

George Barton lived in Boardman during the Depression. He taught in Boardman in 1917 and was once the school Superintendent. He remembers the Hitchcock homestead at Market Street and Route 224. It was a big farm. It was probably the best equipped of any farm around They made the hay down where the Plaza is, hauled it up, and put it in a big barn up near the center. The Hitchcock house was a beautiful place on the corner. It was wood and painted white.

Elton Beard- I had to ride a pony all year to school. I used to park the pony up at the center where Morgan's restaurant is. There used to be a barn and I tied the pony there and then walked down to the school. On the fire department- Mr. Gifford was the Chief of the fire department and this is my first memory of this when I lived on California Drive. We didn't have a regular truck; we had just a cart with spare equipment on it. We had only volunteer firemen, of course, and when the whistle would go, the volunteers would come. Then Troyers across the street had a feed store and they would bring their truck over and hitch their truck to the slow cart and that's the way we would go out to a fire.

George Bohn- School teacher, Dean of Boys and Volunteer Fireman- When I first went to school, I rode in a horse-drawn school bus and I lived on the corner of Tippecanoe Road and Route 224 on a 460 acre farm. There was a blacksmith shop, the Jack Hallett shop, and I used to drive a team of horses up there.

John Darnell Sr. – Originated The Boardman News. Born in 1920. When asked about the biggest fires he says "I think the greatest attention getter happened at Southern Park, when Jenkins' barn caught fire. He had a lot of riding horses out there, and I can't honestly remember how many horses were killed. The barn was practically destroyed. There was another fire of that type on the corner of Tippecanoe and 224. Mrs. Hebberding's barn caught on fire. That killed some cattle and destroyed the barn completely.

Did the people have town meetings? Not too much. Practically all of the meetings were held in the old town hall where we had our office. It wasn't a town hall really; it was a hall for the church, sort of a Fellowship Hall. By the way, the first basketball ever played in the area was played in that old building. To heat the building, they had four pot-bellied stoves, one in each corner.

Judge Harold Doyle- Lived at the corner of Southern Boulevard and Route 224. His family came here in 1906. Market Street was just starting to be graded from the city limits to about a quarter mile past the center. Route 224 was improved after Market Street had been done. They would say that a road has been macadamized or paved with layers of broken stone. Later a street was asphalted over the crushed stone.

The school was just south of the Hitchcock farm on Market Street. The school was a four room frame building. Just south of that was the town hall and south of that was the Methodist Church. After graduating from Boardman, where there were 8 graduates in 1908, I went to the YMCA school which is now Youngstown University.

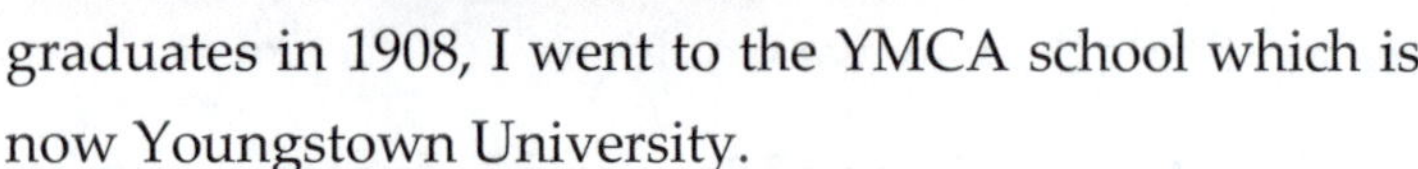

Pearl Gleckler Doyle- In talking about a dance hall she mentions Bannowbrook as being back in the woods off of Market Street.

There was a roof over the whole thing but there were no windows or sides. Jack Hallett's blacksmith shop was located on the southeast corner of Market Street and Route 224 opposite the Hitchcock farm (on the Southern Park Mall property).

Lou Fenton- the owner of Fenton's Service Station located directly across from the Boardman School. He worked for the Township as an equipment operator. When asked about stores he said, "The first that I remember was right in Boardman. It was Gifford's. He was across the tracks on 224 about where the Boardman Supply is now. The first fire truck was stashed alongside Gifford's store. It was just a Model T Ford with some ladders and a bunch of buckets. They had a bucket brigade in those days. When Hitchcock's had the fire, we had a bucket brigade trying to put it out."

John Drennan- Township Constable When asked if there were any big fires he responded, "One big fire was at the plaza right before Christmas in 1953. Stambaugh was opening a big branch to show their appliances. It caught on fire. I was the first one there before the fire department or anything. People were flocking in there in cars to get a front row seat to watch the fire. I tried to keep cars from coming in so the fire trucks could get through. When they came down, I was standing in the middle of the road and the deputy sheriff's car came rolling down on 224 which was a two lane road. Thank goodness it was because they had no siren and I just happened to turn around and see them heading straight for me. I dove into the ditch at the side of the road. The firemen were just unwrapping their hose when the gas in the store caused an explosion and blew out the windows. Five minutes later the firemen would have been in there and possibly killed.

William Dressel moved to Boardman in 1919. - When asked about fires he said, "We did have a fire when the race track burnt up. Which was right on the corner of McClurg and this was before Southern

Boulevard was in. There was a fire there that would run up all the horses and the barns at the race track which was quite an extent. Because of the fact that right after Boardman just got their first fire truck which was a Model T Ford and with no road available, they had to carry it across the swamp to get to the fire. So, it was quite an unusual thing. I got there after the fire started and we helped get the horses out as much as we could. We ran them out as fast as we could. The firemen worked on the fire as fast as they could. Without water it was real trouble, in fact, we lost practically all our horses.

Armen Garver was born in 1918 – The streetcar that went to the race track had a huge waiting room (roof) that was 200′ long and 20′ wide where hundreds of people could stand inside in the rain to wait on the streetcars to take them to the track. My dad tells me when he was young, he saw the first airplane come out there and he crashed up there. It was one of those old fashioned planes.

Jockeys from the Southern Park Racetrack used to board at the Garver farm across from McClurg Road and Market Street. Armen Garver and his brother slept on the floor in the living room because their bedroom had been rented. The boys were not permitted to go to the racetrack so they used to climb to the top of the windmill that was on the farm and watch the races from there. After the Southern Park closed and began to deteriorate, the Garvers helped to tear down the grandstands, small buildings, and horse barns. Many of the boards from those buildings were taken to their farm. The Garver house today has two by fours in it that were once part of some of the racetrack barns.

Mrs. Robert Grove – Do you remember any kinds of businesses in the town? I remember, especially, a grocery store where we always bought our groceries from out here in Boardman. It was Gifford's store. When we first went there, it was just a small building on the other side of the Y and S tracks, the southeast corner, just a small building. Later on, it moved across the tracks to the northwest corner, and the thing I remember about it always, a lot of people in those days didn't pay cash for their groceries. They'd carry a bill and settle it up at the end of one week or two weeks. Whenever you paid your bill, Mr. Gifford gave you a big sack of candy.

Judge Elwyn Jenkins - Were there any bad sections or roads in which there were many accidents? Well, the worst one would be the Midlothian and Market Street, where it used to be what is called the S-curve. The road went straight by Newport Theater, then jogged over to where the Midlothian and Market intersection is now, and then went into the city. That S-curve is as bad an intersection as we had.

Ivor Jenkins- Park Superintendent and Volunteer Fireman The Y & S ran tandem trolleys to the racetrack sometimes to take care of the crowds coming to Southern Park. There was a saloon at Meadowbrook and Market and there was a brewery way out on Hitchcock Road that made some good stuff. We walked everywhere. A good friend had a horse-drawn sleigh that was a wagon that they put sled runners on. A friend of mine had to be taken to the hospital and was taken in this sleigh. In the Depression, we would go out into the coal mines and dig our own coal to heat our houses.

David Kaiser – Do you know where the first fire station was? The first fire station was down on Southern Boulevard on U. S. 224. That's the first one I remember. It was strictly a volunteer fire station. Mr. Merle Gifford, who owned the grocery store, was the Fire Chief. And we had one fire truck I think. The fire station was right next to the store. Being a fireman was voluntary. But because of the sincereness of the Chiefs, such as Mr. Gifford, as I remember, they had schooling. You went about once a week and you were trained. You were taught how to perform rescues, how to perform artificial respiration, how to take care of bandaging people who were injured, and how to lift them and put them onto a stretcher to take them away. They did a great deal of teaching. They had an American LaFrance fire truck. We were very proud of that truck. It was always well taken care of. That was the only piece of equipment that I can remember in those days. I don't remember any of the older equipment. Mr. Hallett had a farm directly across from us at 34 Boardman Poland Road He milked cows and raised corn and wheat. He was a blacksmith who had a blacksmith shop on the corner of 224 and Market Street

Julie Kennell, a teacher, moved to Boardman in 1927 – We came from Youngstown to Boardman to live in the country because of my father's tuberculosis. We were always city people. We lived right across from the Agnew farm. We couldn't believe how the kids dressed in school. They had the same outfits that they wore to milk the cows. Many of them smelled like a farm but they were nice kids. Many of them became well known people in Boardman. Some gypsies came to Boardman. We used to go to the gypsy camp. It was down beyond the Agnew and Pugh farm. They used to settle there. We used to go down there and watch them dance. It was entertainment.

Hugh Manchester- Park Commissioner, lawyer lived here since 1910 - I remember Market Street when half of it was brick and the other half was macadam. Have you ever heard of Dead Man's Curve? In those days, Market Street did not angle off at Midlothian, it went right straight past what is now Newport Theater and intersected Midlothian there, and then you had to turn to the east for a short distance to go down Market Street That was called Dead Man's Curve because there were so many accidents, people hurt and killed at that intersection. I remember the night the Hitchcock barn burned. Mrs. Frank Ewing called us about midnight; Mrs. Manchester's father and mother were with us that time upon Elm Street. As we went out to the car, we could see the light up in the sky from the fire. The barn was destroyed, some cattle, some horses.

Steve Perry- Service Station owner and Volunteer Fireman. I was a fireman for 30 years. The best events of the year were the firemen having a water battle. It was a lot of fun, getting your boots filled with water and of course, it was in the summertime. There were usually many fire department events along with a picnic.

Carl Ruckenbrod lived on Walker Mill Road. When we moved to Boardman from Beaver Township, my dad bought 125 acres and there was a barn and he was a pretty good handyman. He built more to the house, the kitchen, and a shed that we used to raise hogs and keep corn in like a crib. He went to school with Orville Slagle. For entertainment, there were "box socials." The girls would pack a box with food and take it to where the party was being held and they would auction it off. The person who bought the box got to eat lunch with the girl who brought the box.

Where did the teenagers hang out? The Boardman Fire Station was born during my younger days and later on, quite a few guys hung around there. We used to pitch horseshoes there and there was a fellow called Cope Hall. He chewed Copenhagen snuff so we called him Cope. He was the champion horseshoe pitcher.

Were you familiar with the Southern Park Racetrack? Yes, there was a huge grandstand with its back toward McClurg Road (only about 50') facing north and the track was north of that. It was a ½ mile track and there was a famous horse buried there. They were all harness horses in those days. There was a very fine dance pavilion that included a confectionary where I had my first ice cream cone, 5 cents for a scoop of ice cream. The only flavors were vanilla and chocolate. They had some outstanding orchestras and I recall the Mason-Dixon Nine and Red Nichols. It was a pretty good pavilion. The dancehall was further north than the racetrack. The grandstand, then the track oval, and the barns were next. Further into the woods, the pavilion was located and it was about ¼ mile from McClurg Road I don't think it was anywhere near as big as Idora Park Ballroom but it was a good size and very attractive. It was located in a large grove of trees and lots of horse stables. There was another dance hall called the Bannowbrook. It was right on Market Street approximately across from the location of the outdoor theater, at the corner of Washington Boulevard and Market Street. They called it Bannowbrook Dancing Under The Stars. We had a man who played bass tuba, who was called Tiny Harris. He

ish of a trotting race at Southern Park, 1916

was 345 pounds of harmony. He was the greatest bass player and a fine tenor singer. Have you heard about the race between an airplane and an automobile at the track? The old fashioned bi-plane and an automobile raced each other just for kicks. They had a race on the oval, and the airplane won but by a very small margin. The restrooms were a long walk down the woods.

Do you recall any businesses? The only store was the old Gifford and Laucks' grocery store. That was the location of the Boardman Supply Company and a man by the name of Merle Gifford became the Fire Chief and I think then went to Austintown and has now retired from there. Gifford and Laucks' had a store that I don't believe was any bigger than a double garage and was built pretty much the same as a double garage with a hip roof. Then, they sold gas out front and it had a pretty good supply of groceries. It became quite a hangout, in fact. I was one of the first three bus drivers in Boardman, and the bus driver always stopped in at Gifford and Laucks' for a drink of pop on their way home from school. There were no Township owned buses, we owned the bus and used it for farm purposes when we weren't using it to haul kids. There were seats on both sides and one seat down the middle. We'd take out that one seat down the middle and put whatever we wanted into it: potatoes, wheat, corn. But we used it as a piece of farm equipment and a school bus. Carl describes the streets as macadam, large stones and smaller ones mixed with tar.

Neva Simon – One night, a woman woke me up around midnight, I went outside into the field and when I got to Hitchcock Road, the house across the street where we used to live was on fire. The fire department was called. The fire department came in a little while but when they ran out of water, they went back to Glenwood Avenue to get more but they didn't have a wrench to open the fireplug so they had quite a time getting water and the house was pretty shot.

Mrs. Harold Sittig – The Southern Park race track was still there but I imagine it was used partly then, but later the race was given up. The place was only used as a picnic area. The old people dressed in black and the young dressed in white. A lot of the races were sulky races; a rider sat in a two wheel cart and drove the horses. As children, we always thought that was exciting because we would hope the wheel would lock and there would be a wreck.

About the only thing Boardman preserved, was Saint James Church. They saved the old tavern because that was on the northeast corner and it became a Catholic church. Saint Charles and part of it was moved down to the location by 224. It's an ugly building but it's so unique because it's been added to so many times.

Harold Slagle- Volunteer Fireman who lived in Boardman since 1909. Our farm had 155 acres of land and we milked about thirty five head of cattle. We went to school in a horse and wagon until the third grade and then they had one school bus. It was an old truck with cloth side curtains and it held about thirty or thirty five students. Sometimes we started at daylight and if we happened to have a detour, which we did have to because dirt roads were being built into macadamized roads or brick roads. Market Street had one lane of brick and one lane of mud road for the buggies and horses. There was a little swimming hole right about where the plaza is now where we used to take a swim at lunch break and hurry back to school by 12:30.

Do you know anything about the Southern Racetrack? Yes, quite a lot because when I was a kid I used to park cars there. People came from all over this part of the state of Ohio. It consisted of the race track, and the big grandstand, it was really big for those days, they had a nice baseball field, they had a very large dance hall for that time and Youngstown and Southern streetcars ran from Youngstown out. They would be so crowded, people were hanging all over the cars and they ran about every ten minutes to bring people out from Youngstown. They had motorcycle races, automobile races, dog races, horse races, trotter pacers, and regular running races. I remember a horse that dropped dead just before the finish of a race, he was a very famous horse but can't recall his name, so he was buried in the center of the race track, with a flagpole there.

Were there any bad fires in Boardman? Yes, there were some bad fires; they didn't have the equipment at that time to fight the fires, the water lines weren't run scarcely anywhere and at the time, they were mostly farm fires. At the present site of the Sohio Station at the corner of 224 and Market Street, there was a large farm owned by the Hitchcock family and they had a tremendous barn. The barn burnt and in those days everyone had cattle, a lot of cattle burned up and there were farm fires around this area and at the time, they figured there was a farm firebug in this area, but he was never located, and eventually, we quit having them.

The fire department was all volunteers. The first fire truck was on an old Model T Ford and there was room for a couple to sit in the front with the driver and there was a step on the back where people could stand, but it didn't go very fast and if it hit a bump, your feet bounced off the back step and you were running behind and you had to jump back on. We had that probably for about ten years.

Were there any prominent people in Boardman? Below me here (8419 South Avenue.), about 500 yards, there was a schoolhouse where President McKinley taught school for a short period of time, one or two years. He was born in Niles and moved to Poland where he taught school here. This house was built in 1933, but we have a large family here. There are four houses of Slagles in a row.

Harold & Orville Sagle

Orville Slagle- Volunteer Fireman lived in Boardman back in the horse and buggy days. I went to school in a horse and wagon and in the wintertime, we used to go on the horse and bobsleigh. I graduated from Boardman in 1924. Do you remember Agnew's potato patch? Yes, I remember the Agnews. They had a barn burn down one time.

Were you here when the first car came about? Yes, I can remember the first car I ever saw. It was one of my mother's relations in Cleveland who owned it. It was around here that I saw an automobile. When they sent us word that they were coming down, us kids would watch down the road all day long to see that car coming. Finally, late that afternoon, they came. It was an open car with the gear shifts on the outside of the body on the fender, you had to reach out and shift the gears. The lights on the car in those days were gas. You had to carry a tank of gas on the car and it was piped up to the headlights. And when you were out at night, you had to get out and turn the tank on and run in front and light it with a match.

Did anything happen around Boardman like a fire? Yes, we would have fires once in a while. There was one big one I remember when I got out of school. It was after I got married. That was about 45 years ago when the big barn on Hitchcock farm burned down. It was right there where the Standard Oil Station is on the southwest corner up in the center of Boardman. A lot of cattle burned also. Of course, we had a lot of other barns and houses burn down, the McKay place on the corner of South Avenue and 224. There was a house that burned down two different times and the barn burned once. Back then we had a fire department, but we had no fire hydrants. We had the department that carried the large tank of water and then we were able to pump the water down at McKay's Creek. In the olden days, we had the bucket brigade and they would get a whole row of people from the pump to the fire. And when you would see a fire, you would run with your bucket and all the neighbors came in and they pumped the bucket full of water at the pump and handed up the line. And you would just have a double line going up and a line of empties coming down the line. By the time the bucket got up to the fire, it was half spilled out anyway but that was the best we could do.

The first fire department was located where the cars cross the tracks at Route 224. Merle Gifford was the first Fire Chief. He had a gas station there. And then they built a little fire station behind it. The first thing they ever had was just a two wheel cart with a tank and pump and they would end up pulling it by hand or they could hitch up onto an automobile. Then they came out with the Model T Ford with a couple of chemical things on it. How many men were on the fire department squad? I belonged to it for many years. I don't know at first what we were limited to, but I know when I dropped off of it, they were limited to 25 men and they were volunteers and they didn't get paid then. Before I dropped off, I think they got something like a dollar an hour. The reason I dropped off was because I was way down here and a lot of time I didn't hear the siren and I wouldn't get to the fires. And I was just tampering with someone else from getting on because 25 was the limit. So, when I dropped off, it was letting someone else get on who was closer to it.

In 1903- Route 224 looking east is named Ohio Avenue.

What made you become a volunteer fireman? I knew all of the guys that were on there. They were a good bunch and I thought I would like to join them. Do you know how long it took to get the average fire out? I guess it wasn't too long, because if you didn't get to it, it burnt down. We saved a lot of places. I remember one time when that old Model T was there on a Sunday and Gifford was there in his store, and a call came in. And there was a fire down by Woodland and Lockland and only he and I was there. And he said you go out and ring the siren and that was when we just had a button on a pole, and if nobody is here by the time I get the store locked, you and I'll go. So, there was nobody there and it was early Sunday noon and everybody was sleeping in so he and I started on that old Model T. We headed toward McKay's corner and up that way because Southern Boulevard wasn't finished down there then. Then I remember going through a lot of the street and it was rough. And he was driving and I was on the back of the truck and the ladder flew off and ended up in the ditch. And I hollered at him and he couldn't hear me and then he got back there and asked what the matter was. Where are the ladders? And I said they are way out there in the ditch. But we got the fire out of the house, but the people had gone to church and the neighbors had called but we got it out. We used to get a lot of houses out.

Can you describe the fire station? It wasn't nothing much more than a garage, that's all it was, a one car garage. Did anybody ever get seriously hurt in any fires? In Boardman, I can never remember anyone getting seriously hurt.

I remember my parents telling me that William McKinley used to teach school here about a quarter of a mile from here. It was a little country schoolhouse.

Thomas Smith- Volunteer Fireman, Dairy Farmer When he was a young boy, there were no hard surfaced roads. Shields Road at that time started at the intersection of Hopkins Road and went east to Market Street. Our present home now was Bill Lynn's sugar camp. My father and uncle had a dairy farm and it started at the corner of Shields and Tippecanoe. The original barn, on that property, burned around 1910. The sparks from the steam engine set the straw on fire and it got into the barn and burned it. The name of the business was Smith Brothers Shadeland Dairy.

At the Southern Park Racetrack, the baseball field was to the north of the racetrack. Between the two were at least two tennis courts. The Y&S had a turnaround for the trolley cars at the race track stop. The racetrack closed in part because the blue laws in Ohio began to become prominent. They closed all betting. It seems you can't make horse races pay unless you can bet. Frank Hitchcock had his own private half mile track where the plaza is now. I remember that 4 or 5 barnstorming planes came to the Southern Park Racetrack and put on an act and gave people rides for $5.

What kind of fire protection did we have in Boardman? Boardman has the best fire protection or equal to any in the state or any city. At one time we had all three Trustees that were firemen and it was all voluntary fire department at that time. We had regular meetings once a month and a drill every Monday night and they put on quite a few social gatherings; fish fries and different things to raise money but the people in the Township were kind to the fire department whenever they asked for millage to buy new equipment or anything. I don't ever remember them being turned down consequently, Boardman after they got going, had better and newer equipment than Youngstown had. They had a two-way radio before Youngstown had it. There was no fire department in the state that was better than Boardman.

Before our present department, what was there in the way of fire protection? Nothing except you took care of your own and when there was a fire, the neighbors came streaming in and grabbed all the furniture and threw it outside, it didn't matter if it was raining or not, out it went. At a neighbor's house down the road, people named Hopkins, which was an old family here in Boardman, their house caught on fire and they saved two things, they saved the piano which they brought up to our house in a wagon in the rain and stored it at our house until they rebuilt and someone went in and jerked the telephone off the wall and saved it and it belonged to the telephone company.

In Tom Smith's Junior year, he and Marshall Fisher were at a BBQ restaurant and overheard a boy from South High talking about his school yearbook. When they got back to school, they asked Mr. Henderson if they could start a yearbook and he said that he thought Boardman was big enough to have its own yearbook and so from there is how the yearbook started. They had started the Boardman Crier.

Mrs. Tannehill spent summers at Bannowbrook Estate many summers – Describes how, after the owner, Mr. Roche died, the property was leased to a promoter who built the dance area. It is described as a shell for the band and an open area wooden dance floor. This was from 1931 to 1945.

She also describes that in the summers, the Ku Klux Klan would gather across from the home at the spot where the drive-in theater was and she could see them from her bedroom window. There would be many many white hooded people roaming around and then in due time two or three large crosses would be put up and lit. To me, she said, this was terrifying and it was a great trauma. This happened every month in the summer for many years.

1918 Horse Drawn
Boardman School Bus.

1930 Boardman School Bus.

In a series of historical documents written by Esther Feight in 1953, she writes:

The first paved road in Boardman Township, in fact in Mahoning County, (outside of Youngstown) was Boardman Road (now Market Street) from Hill's Corners (now Midlothian Boulevard) to Boardman Center. John Hitchcock was one of the men who used his influence to get county roads improved. Boardman Road was paved with brick and only the east half of it was paved in about 1907.

It was hard for horses to travel on paving, so if the roads were good, people preferred to drive on dirt. Gradually automobiles were beginning to travel the roads. When anyone was driving with a horse on the brick part, they were supposed to turn off into the dirt part regardless of the direction they were going. Of course, that might happen only occasionally or not at all. Usually, after the driver did turn off onto the dirt road, he had to get out and hold the horse by the bit in his mouth until the auto passed. Even then, chances were that the horse would rear up in the air. Horses were so afraid of these horseless carriages which made so much noise and were such high, gawky looking apparatuses.

In 1953, Boardman's population was about 15,000. Boardman was the most densely populated Township in the State of Ohio, which is not incorporated and under Township government. Recently, (September 30, 1953 report date) the Trustees succeeded in getting a bill passed in the legislature in

Columbus which gives the Trustees more power to furnish more police protection to our growing community.

On our streets: Some of the streets in Boardman have been named after the early settlers: Simon Road, Ewing Road, Hitchcock Road, Hopkins Road,

McClurg Road, Boardman Boulevard, Stilson Place, Shields Road, Simon Road, Brainard Drive, Newton Avenue, Withers Drive, Newport Drive, Titus, and Marinthiana Avenue.

James Shields Prominent Cattleman

James H. Shields was born in Canfield Township in 1840 and were reared in Boardman attending Boardman schools. It is reported that in 1859 he taught school here. From the time he was 12 years of age until he reached 19 he drove cattle during the "season" which ran from April to September.

At the age of 13, he went to Illinois to purchase 200 head of cattle for which he paid $7,000. He drove the cattle back east, through Youngstown, finally reaching his destination, Hudson, New York in 87 days. There he sold his cattle. At the outbreak of the Civil War he was the first man to enlist in the first company raised at Youngstown, eventually becoming a general in that company, the 7th Ohio Regiment of Volunteer Infantry. From 1898 to 1900 he was elected as the Mahoning County Sheriff.

James H. Shields

David Simon

1918 David Simon's farm was near the intersection of Simon Road and Indianola Road. He managed a very successful dairy and crop farm.

BUSINESS DIRECTORY—BOARDMAN TOWNSHIP.

J. H. GOOD, Saw Mill and Lumber Dealer. Post-office address, Poland.

GEORGE HORNIKEL, Farmer. Makes a specialty of Cream, Butter and Eggs. Post office address, Poland.

JAMES A. BROWNLEE & SONS, General Farmers and Dealers in Horned Cattle. Post-office address, Poland.

B. S. MATHEWS, Farmer and Breeder of Delaine Sheep. Post-office address, Poland.

DAVID B. RAYMOND, Postmaster and Store-keeper, Stationery, Tobacco and Cigars. Post-office address, Boardman Centre.

S. E. SLAGLE, Farmer and Agent for Harvesting and Farm Machinery. Post-office address, Poland.

ZENIX McCLURE, Manager and Farmer for the Hitchcock Stock Farm. Post-office address, Boardman Centre.

GEORGE BALDWIN, General Farmer and Stock Breeder, Boardman Road.

NORTH NEWTON, Proprietor Grist Mill in Poland Borough. Residence, Boardman Centre.

WM. RIPLEY, General Farmer. GEO. W. RIPLEY, Saw and Planing Mill, Dealer in all kinds of Hard Wood and Native Lumber for Building purposes. Post-office address, Boardman Centre, Boardman Township, Ohio.

MRS. LUCY A. BALDWIN, widow of the late Jessie Baldwin, one of the well-known citizens of Mahoning County. Residence, Boardman Centre, Boardman Township, Ohio.

GEORGE H. DAVIDSON, General Farmer and Produce Grower. Post-office address, Boardman Centre, Ohio.

CHAS. A. MESSERLY, Indian and Mill Creek Stock Farm and Dairy, Breeder of Short-Horns and Thoroughbreds. Farm in Boardman Township. Residence, Canfield, Ohio.

JACOB BAISLER, Overlook Farm, General Farmer and Dairyman. Colt Breeding a specialty. Post-office address, Poland. Residence, Boardman Township, Ohio.

Maple sugar gathering was an annual chore for the early Boardman pioneers. Above members of the Simon family gather sap from trees to be made into sugar-water and molasses. This picture was taken around 1900, probably during February or March when the sugar season began in earnest.

About The Author

I enjoyed a 42 year career with Boardman Fire Department starting as a volunteer firefighter in 1968 and retiring in 2011. I spent my early years as a training officer, and eight years as Captain, which put me on the rescue squad during that time. I spent another eight years as an Assistant Chief. I was appointed to the position of Fire Chief and remained in that position for fifteen years until my retirement.

My wife, Sandy and I raised three girls in Boardman Ohio. I followed my girls through their soccer experience, coaching them from youth soccer to high school soccer. I eventually made my way to head coach of the Varsity soccer team for eight years.

In retirement, we have enjoyed spending time traveling, visiting family and friends all around the country, and dividing our time between Ohio and Florida.

I thoroughly enjoyed talking with the retired and current firefighters as I documented their stories about fighting some of the biggest fires Boardman had experienced over the years. Through these books, their stories will be remembered for generations to come.

Made in the USA
Columbia, SC
19 April 2025